The Ultimate Backseat Book

kids' road atlas

Contents

Using an Atlas...

Adventure or Mystery?

Is map reading an adventure or a mystery? It's only a mystery if you haven't uncovered the clues and codes. The information below will help you unlock the mystery and get started on the adventure. Solve the clues and use the numbered letters to fill in the secret message. For some of the clues you'll need to use the legend, scale, and coordinates, but for others you'll have to do a bit more detective work. Take a closer look at the maps for familiar cities, bordering states, and other details to help you find the answers. Good luck!

Map Legend

Road symbols		City symbols		Other symbols	
▬▬▬	Freeway or Tollway	★	National capital	■	Point of interest
───	Highway	✪	State capital	▲	Mountain peak
40	Interstate highway	●	City or town		Park area
65	U.S. highway				Lake or reservoir
40	Canadian highways	**Map symbols**		───	River or canal
1	Mexican highway	0 10 mi. / 0 10 km.	Map Scale	▬▬	State boundary
15 9	State or provincial highways	N	North Arrow		

Legend

The legend, or map key, is a description of the symbols and lines on the map. Use the legend at the left for all of the maps in *Kids' Road Atlas*.

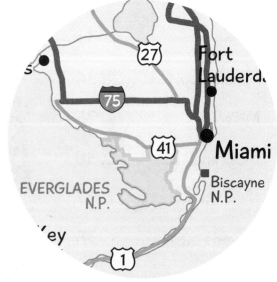

Clue #1: What National Park (N.P.) is at the southernmost section of the map at the right?

___ ___ ___ ___ ___ ___ ___ ___ ___ N.P.
        1   2

Clue #2: In what state will you find this park?

___ ___ ___ ___ ___ ___ ___
            3   4

Scale

Maps come in all sizes. Some show the whole world and others show only a small neighborhood. The map scale tells you how space on a map equals distance on the earth. Scale is used to measure distances between places on a map. Measure the length of the distance from place to place on the map and then use the scale to find out how many miles or kilometers that is. The maps in Kids' Road Atlas are not all at the same scale, so be sure to look at the scale on each map to measure distance correctly.

Clue #3: On the map at the right, what "mile-high" city is approximately 30 miles southeast of Boulder on Interstate 25?

___ ___
5   6

Clue #4: In what state will you find these two cities?

___ ___
7   8

Coordinates

A coordinate is a letter–number combination that helps you find places on a map. To locate a city, look in the index to find the coordinate for that city. If, for example, the coordinate for the city is B–5, look down the right or left edge of the map for the letter B and draw an imaginary line across the map. Then, look across the top or bottom of the map for the number 5 and draw an imaginary line down or up until it meets the imaginary line drawn from the letter B. The city will be inside the area around this point. For each map in the *Kids' Road Atlas* there is an orange coordinate border with letters and numbers.

Clue #5: What coastal city on the map below is at coordinate H–5? Hint: There are several, so make sure you pick the one that fits in the blanks.

___ ___ ___   ___ ___   ___
⑨ ⑩ 11   12   13

Clue #6: In what state is this city located?

___ ___ ___   ___ ___
14   15

Clue #7: You'll find this Mexican city at coordinate I–5.

___ ___ ___   ___
16   ⑰   ⑱

Have you solved all the clues? Congratulations! Use the letters from the numbered spaces in your answers to figure out this secret message:

___ ___ ___   ___ ___ ___ ___ ___ ___ ___ ___ ___
16 13   5   18   4   6   5 15 16 17   8   5

___ ___ ___ ___ ___ ___   ___ ___ ___ ___   ___   ___ ___ ___ ___
12   5   1   3 15   2   10   3 16 13   18   16 17   8 15

___ ___   ___ ___ ___   ___ ___ ___ ___!
7 14   16 13   5   11 18   1   5

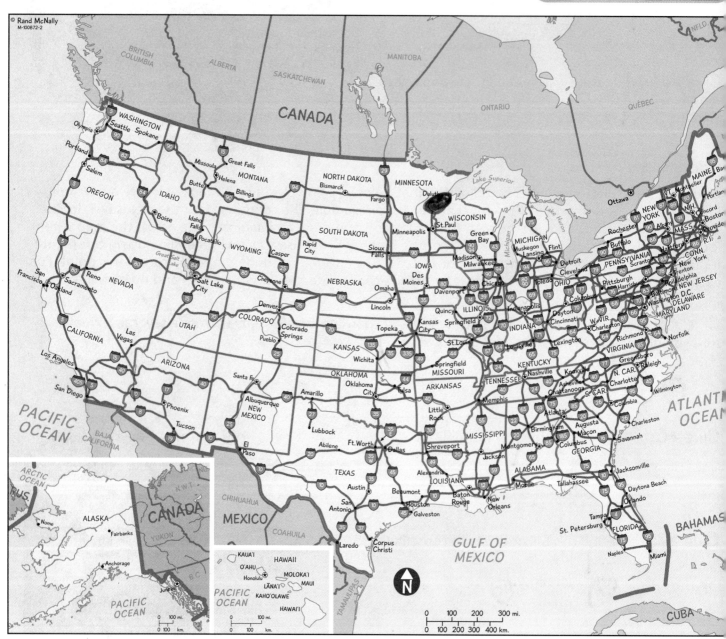

Keep it Brief

Each state has a two-letter abbreviation. On the next page, write the abbreviation for each state in the blanks provided. Remember that the two-letter abbreviation should be written in capital letters. Hint: Check out the state names in the red bar at the top of the pages in this book. The two letters of the abbreviation are the two capital letters in the name.

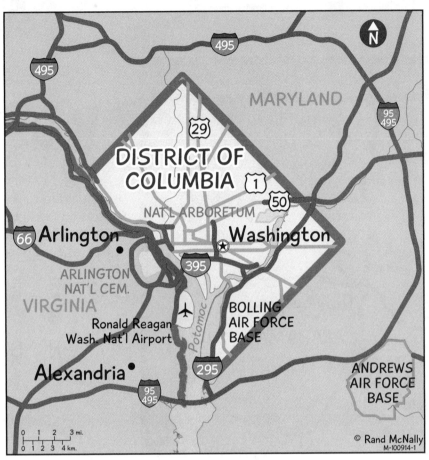

1. __A__ Alabama
2. __A__ Alaska
3. __A__ Arizona
4. __A__ Arkansas
5. __C__ California
6. __C__ Colorado
7. ____ Connecticut
8. ____ Delaware
9. ____ Florida
10. ____ Georgia
11. ____ Hawaii
12. ____ Idaho
13. ____ Illinois
14. ____ Indiana
15. ____ Iowa
16. ____ Kansas
17. ____ Kentucky

18. ____ Louisiana
19. ____ Maine
20. ____ Maryland
21. ____ Massachusetts
22. ____ Michigan
23. ____ Minnesota
24. ____ Mississippi
25. ____ Missouri
26. ____ Montana
27. ____ Nebraska
28. ____ Nevada
29. ____ New Hampshire
30. ____ New Jersey
31. ____ New Mexico
32. ____ New York
33. ____ North Carolina
34. ____ North Dakota

35. ____ Ohio
36. ____ Oklahoma
37. ____ Oregon
38. ____ Pennsylvania
39. ____ Rhode Island
40. ____ South Carolina
41. ____ South Dakota
42. ____ Tennessee
43. ____ Texas
44. ____ Utah
45. ____ Vermont
46. ____ Virginia
47. ____ Washington
48. ____ West Virginia
49. ____ Wisconsin
50. ____ Wyoming

ALabama

Nickname: The Heart of Dixie | **Capital:** Montgomery

Southern pine | Camellia | Yellowhammer

© Rand McNally
M-100855-1

TENNESSEE

Florence 72
Huntsville
Decatur 231 72
43 65 59
Guntersville Lake 411
22 Gadsden
20
Birmingham
ALABAMA
Tuscaloosa
Martin Lake
82 231
20 59 Auburn
Demopolis 80 85
84 Montgomery 82
331
65 431
Jackson Andalusia 84
43 29 Dothan
Mobile FLORIDA
10 59
GULF OF MEXICO

MISSISSIPPI | GEORGIA

0 10 20 mi.
0 10 20 30 km.

BLAST OFF!

Use the code to discover where the Space and Rocket Center is located. Write the correct letters in the blanks at the bottom of the page.

A	B	E	H	I	L

M	N	S	T	U	V

AlasKa

Sitka spruce  | Forget-me-not | Willow ptarmigan

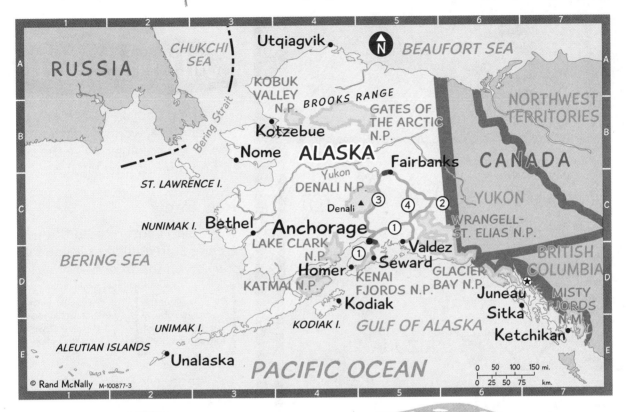

© Rand McNally   M-100877-3

DiSCOVeriNG aLaSKa

Circle the Alaska words in the grid.

ANCHORAGE
BALD EAGLE
DOG SLED RACE
ESKIMO
GLACIER
GOLD
GRIZZLY BEAR
IGLOO
JUNEAU
KAYAK

MOOSE
MOUNTAIN
OTTER
SALMON
SNOW
TREE
REINDEER
TUNDRA
WATERFALL
WHALE

K	L	L	A	F	R	E	T	A	W	M	O
B	A	L	D	E	A	G	L	E	S	O	A
S	U	Y	L	T	R	E	E	N	L	O	N
R	A	E	A	T	D	L	O	G	O	S	C
E	E	L	S	K	N	W	I	L	M	E	H
E	N	G	M	O	U	N	T	A	I	N	O
D	U	O	T	O	T	O	A	C	K	L	R
N	J	A	S	K	N	T	A	I	S	S	A
I	O	O	W	H	A	L	E	E	E	N	G
E	D	O	G	S	L	E	D	R	A	C	E
R	A	E	B	Y	L	Z	Z	I	R	G	X

AriZona

| Palo verde | | Saguaro cactus blossom | | Cactus wren | |

MiGHtY GRaND

The Grand Canyon (C–2) is one of the seven natural wonders of the world. Its size is incredible! Solve the problems to find out just how big it is.

How Deep?

The Grand Canyon could fit this many Empire State Buildings inside its walls, stacked on top of one another!

$$\left[\begin{array}{c} \text{The number of the} \\ \text{Interstate highway} \\ \text{that runs east-west} \\ \text{through Flagstaff} \end{array} \right] \bigg/ \left[\begin{array}{c} \text{The number of the} \\ \text{Interstate highway} \\ \text{that runs east-west} \\ \text{through Tucson} \end{array} \right] = $$

$$\underline{\qquad} \bigg/ \underline{\qquad} = \underline{\qquad}$$

How Long?

The Grand Canyon is this many miles long—almost the same as the width of the state of Utah!

$$\left[\begin{array}{c} \text{The number} \\ \text{of the} \\ \text{U.S highway} \\ \text{that runs} \\ \text{down} \\ \text{Arizona's} \\ \text{eastern} \\ \text{border} \end{array} \right] + \left[\begin{array}{c} \text{The number} \\ \text{of the} \\ \text{state} \\ \text{highway} \\ \text{that} \\ \text{runs from} \\ \text{Globe to} \\ \text{Springerville} \end{array} \right] - \left[\begin{array}{c} \text{The number} \\ \text{of the} \\ \text{Interstate} \\ \text{highway} \\ \text{running} \\ \text{west from} \\ \text{Phoenix} \end{array} \right] + $$

$$\left[\begin{array}{c} \text{The number of the} \\ \text{Interstate highway} \\ \text{that runs north} \\ \text{from Phoenix} \end{array} \right] + \left[\begin{array}{c} \text{The number of the} \\ \text{Interstate highway} \\ \text{that runs from} \\ \text{south of Tucson} \end{array} \right] = $$

$$=$$

ARkansas

Nickname: The Natural State | **Capital:** Little Rock

Pine  | Apple blossom | Mockingbird

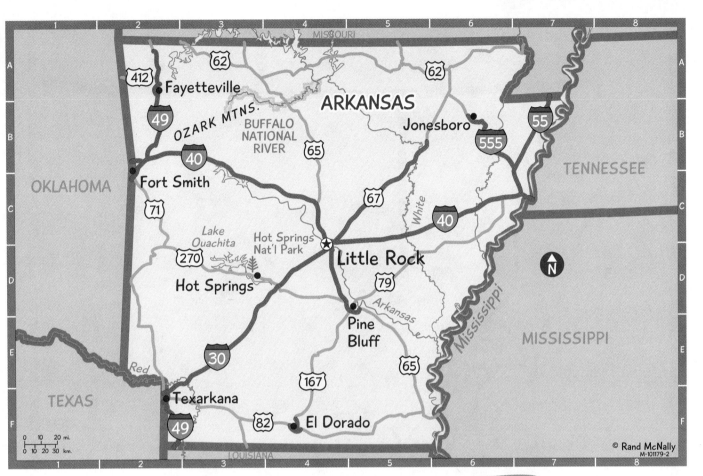

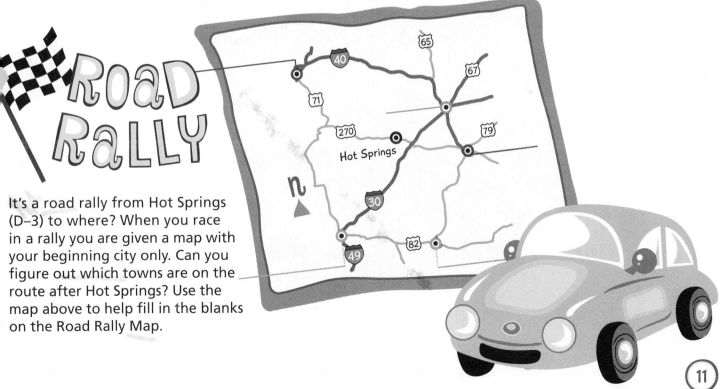

ROAD RALLY

It's a road rally from Hot Springs (D–3) to where? When you race in a rally you are given a map with your beginning city only. Can you figure out which towns are on the route after Hot Springs? Use the map above to help fill in the blanks on the Road Rally Map.

CAlifornia

Nickname: The Golden State | **Capital:** Sacramento

California redwood | Golden poppy | California (valley) quail

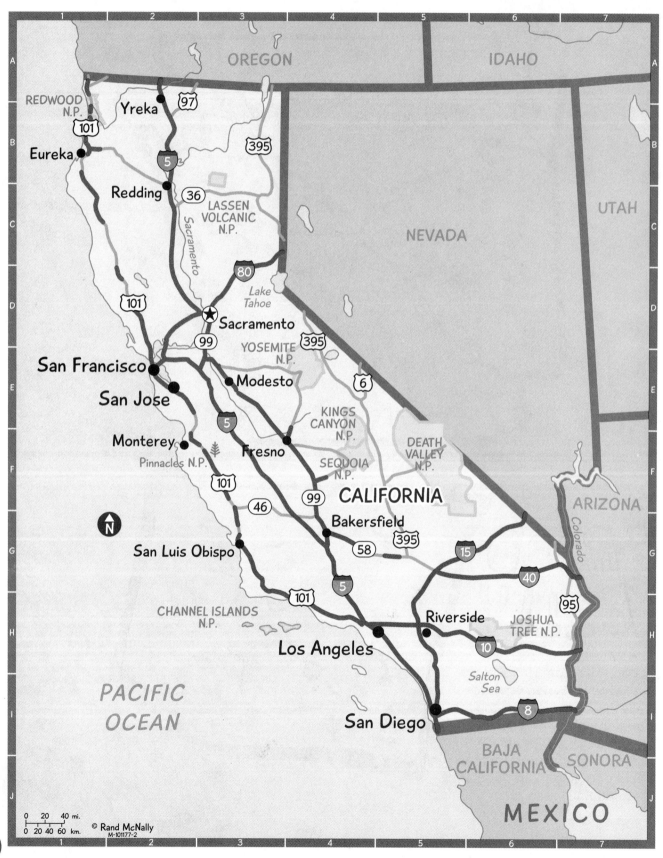

OREGON

IDAHO

REDWOOD N.P.

97

Yreka

101

395

Eureka

5

Redding

36

LASSEN VOLCANIC N.P.

Sacramento (river)

NEVADA

UTAH

80

Lake Tahoe

★ Sacramento

99

395

YOSEMITE N.P.

San Francisco

San Jose

Modesto

6

Monterey

Pinnacles N.P.

5

Fresno

KINGS CANYON N.P.

DEATH VALLEY N.P.

N

101

46

99

SEQUOIA N.P.

CALIFORNIA

ARIZONA

Colorado (river)

San Luis Obispo

Bakersfield

58

395

15

40

95

101

5

CHANNEL ISLANDS N.P.

Riverside

JOSHUA TREE N.P.

Los Angeles

10

PACIFIC OCEAN

Salton Sea

8

San Diego

BAJA CALIFORNIA

SONORA

0 20 40 mi.
0 20 40 60 km.

© Rand McNally
M-101177-2

MEXICO

12

P🌲rk it here

Look at the map of California for the National Parks that are located at the coordinates listed below. Write the names of the parks in the puzzle. The shaded column will spell out California's state motto, reading from top to bottom.

1. B–1
2. F–4
3. H–6
4. D–3
5. E–4
6. F–5

COlorado

Nickname : The Centennial State **Capital :** Denver

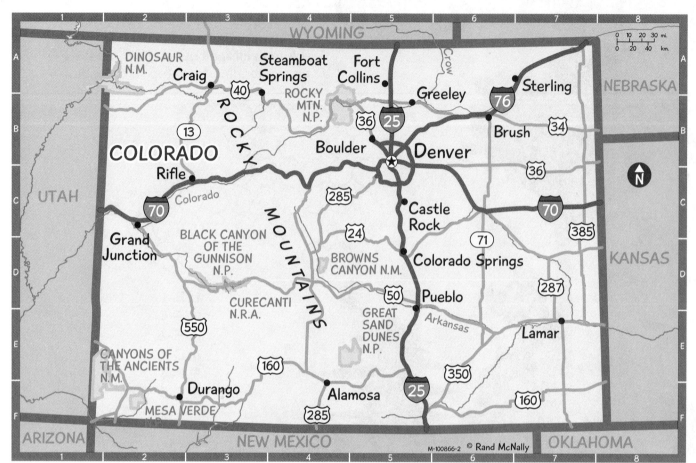

THE NAME GAME

A lot of places in Colorado are named after objects. Look at the pictures below. Can you find the places named after them? Their coordinates are given in parentheses.

B-6

_____

B-5

_____

River   A-6

C-5

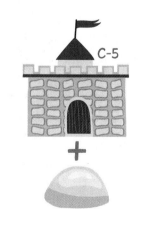

+

_____

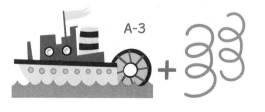

A-3

+

A-2

_____

National Monument

ConnecTicut

Nickname : The Constitution State

Capital : Hartford

White oak | Mountain laurel | American robin

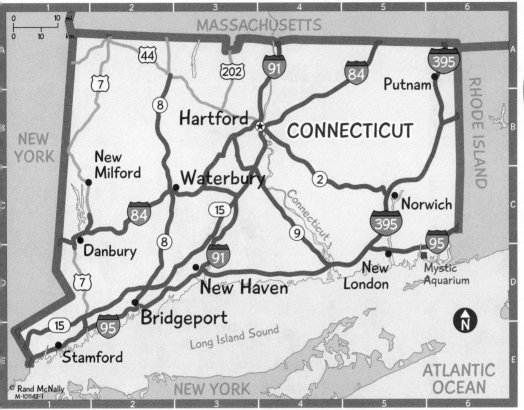

MASSACHUSETTS

44 · 202 · 91 · 84 · Putnam · 395

7 · 8 · Hartford · CONNECTICUT

NEW YORK

New Milford · Waterbury · 2 · Norwich · 395

84 · 15 · 9 · Connecticut · 95

Danbury · 8 · 91 · New London · Mystic Aquarium

7 · New Haven

15 · 95 · Bridgeport · Long Island Sound · N

Stamford

© Rand McNally
M-101142-1

NEW YORK · ATLANTIC OCEAN

RHODE ISLAND

Sea Creature

Color the shapes that contain vowels to find out what's at the Mystic Aquarium (D–5).

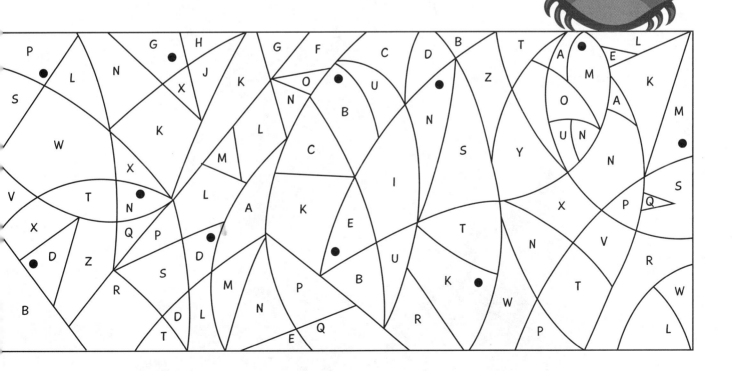

15

DElaware

Nickname: **The First State** | Capital: **Dover**

 American holly |  Peach blossom | Blue hen chicken

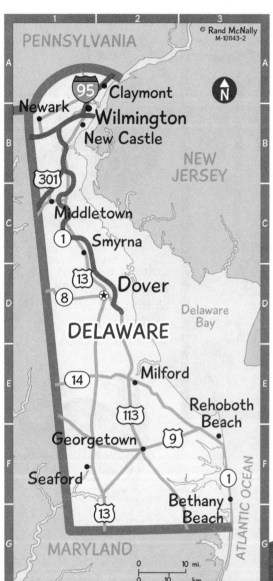

© Rand McNally
M-101143-2

PENNSYLVANIA

Claymont
Newark
Wilmington
New Castle

NEW JERSEY

301
Middletown
Smyrna
13
Dover
8

DELAWARE

Delaware Bay

14 Milford
113 Rehoboth Beach
Georgetown 9
Seaford 1
13 Bethany Beach

ATLANTIC OCEAN

MARYLAND

0   10 mi.
0   10 km.

SHip Shape

Delaware is well-known for its maritime history. Can you spot the correct reflection for this ship?

 16

FLorida

Sabal palm	Orange blossom	Mockingbird

Sit FoR a SpeLL

The Florida beach below shows objects that can be grouped into pairs in which the letters of one thing can be rearranged to spell another. For example, HORSE and SHORE are a pair because they contain the same letters. Rearrange the letters in the words given to make other pairs.

ALABAMA

GEORGIA

Pensacola

Tallahassee

Panama City

Jacksonville

St. Augustine

ATLANTIC OCEAN

Ocala

Daytona Beach

Orlando

Tampa

St. Petersburg

FLORIDA

Lake Okeechobee

FLORIDA'S TPK.

Port St. Lucie

Ft. Myers

Fort Lauderdale

GULF OF MEXICO

EVERGLADES N.P.

Miami

Biscayne National Park

DRY TORTUGAS N.P.

Key West

0 10 20 30 mi.
0 20 40 km.

© Rand McNally
M-100857-1

HORSE _____SHORE_____   MELON _____

OCEAN _____   TEN _____

PALM _____   SHOE _____

PEARS _____   BEARD _____

GeorgiA

Live oak | Cherokee rose | Brown thrasher

Peanuts are an important crop in Georgia. Can you find your way through the peanut maze?

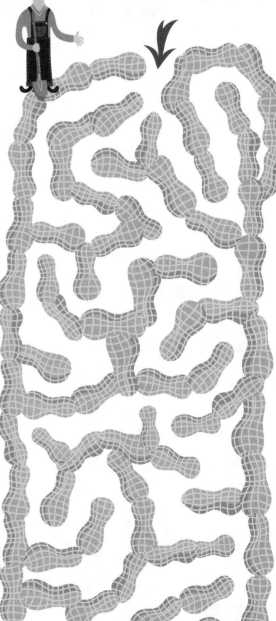

FiNish

Hawaii

Nickname : | Capital :
The Aloha State | Honolulu

Kukui
(candlenut)

Yellow
hibiscus

Nene
(Hawaiian goose)

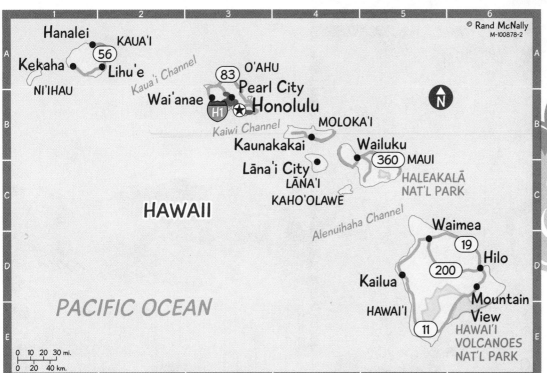

© Rand McNally
M-100878-2

Hanalei
KAUA'I
Kekaha
Lihu'e
NI'IHAU
Kaua'i Channel
83
O'AHU
Wai'anae
Pearl City
H1
Honolulu
Kaiwi Channel
MOLOKA'I
Kaunakakai
Wailuku
360
MAUI
Lāna'i City
HALEAKALĀ
NAT'L PARK
LĀNA'I
KAHO'OLAWE
HAWAII
Alenuihaha Channel
Waimea
19
Hilo
200
Kailua
Mountain
View
HAWAI'I
11
HAWAI'I
VOLCANOES
NAT'L PARK
PACIFIC OCEAN

N

0 10 20 30 mi.
0 20 40 km.

active Hawaii

Connect the dots to find out what
Kilauea is. Kilauea is in the National
Park at coordinate E–6.

IDaho

Nickname :
The Gem State

Capital :
Boise

Western white pine  | Syringa (mock orange) | Mountain bluebird

Idaho is known for growing lots of potatoes. Find 5 potatoes and 5 french fries hidden in this picture of Shoshone Falls (G-3), the "Niagara Falls of the West."

ILlinois

White oak | Native violet  | Cardinal

tour OF iLLiNOiS

Follow the directions for a tour of Illinois. Write the names of the cities you visit as you go.

1. _____
A place to say "Bonjour." (E–5)

2. _____
A place for Santa Claus and Abraham Lincoln. (D–2)

3. _____
A place to have lunch. (B–4)

4. _____
A place to avoid. (B–3)

5. _____
A place to have an average time. (C–4)

6. _____
A place where a poor speller could celebrate. (D–4)

21

INdiana

Nickname: The Hoosier State

Capital: Indianapolis

Tulip tree | Peony | Cardinal

LAKE MICHIGAN

MICHIGAN

Gary

Indiana Dunes Nat'l Park

80 90

South Bend

20

41

30

65

Fort Wayne

ILLINOIS

24

31

69

Lafayette

INDIANA

Anderson

Richmond

74

Indianapolis

70

OHIO

Terre Haute

70

37

Bloomington

74

Columbus

Wabash

50

Vincennes

65

69

150

Ohio

41

64

Evansville

KENTUCKY

© Rand McNally
M-100867-2

A DAY AT THE RACES

In the Indy 500 car race it can be hard to tell who is winning. Some cars can be laps ahead of the others. Use the clues below to figure out which car is winning and which cars are coming in 2nd and 3rd.

1. None of the odd numbered cars finished in the top three.

2. The gray car didn't finish in the top three.

3. The yellow car didn't win.

4. The brown car didn't finish in the top three.

5. The red car came in right behind the orange car.

1st _____

2nd _____

3rd _____

IowA

Oak | Wild rose | Eastern goldfinch

S.D.
MINNESOTA
WISCONSIN
Mason City
Sioux City
Waterloo
Dubuque
IOWA
Ames
Cedar Rapids
Des Moines
Iowa City
Bettendorf
Davenport
NEBRASKA
Council Bluffs
ILLINOIS
Burlington
MISSOURI

© Rand McNally
M-100890-1

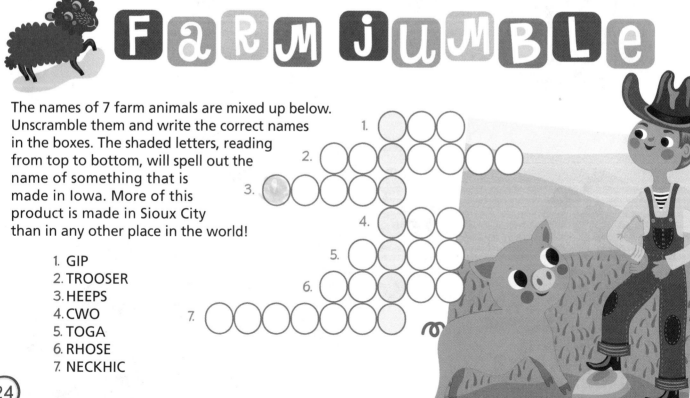

FaRm JumBLe

The names of 7 farm animals are mixed up below. Unscramble them and write the correct names in the boxes. The shaded letters, reading from top to bottom, will spell out the name of something that is made in Iowa. More of this product is made in Sioux City than in any other place in the world!

1. GIP
2. TROOSER
3. HEEPS
4. CWO
5. TOGA
6. RHOSE
7. NECKHIC

1.
2.
3.
4.
5.
6.
7.

24

KanSas

Cottonwood | Native sunflower | Western meadowlark

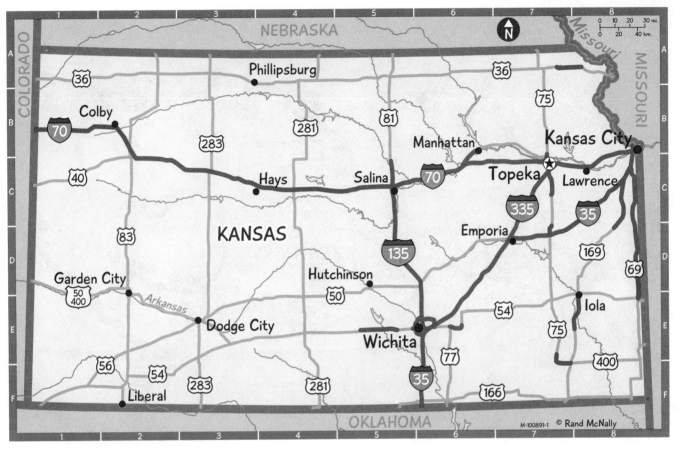

Dodge City, Kansas, was a famous town in the Old West. Circle what doesn't belong in this Old West scene.

KentuckY

Nickname: The Bluegrass State | Capital: Frankfort

Tulip poplar | Goldenrod | Cardinal

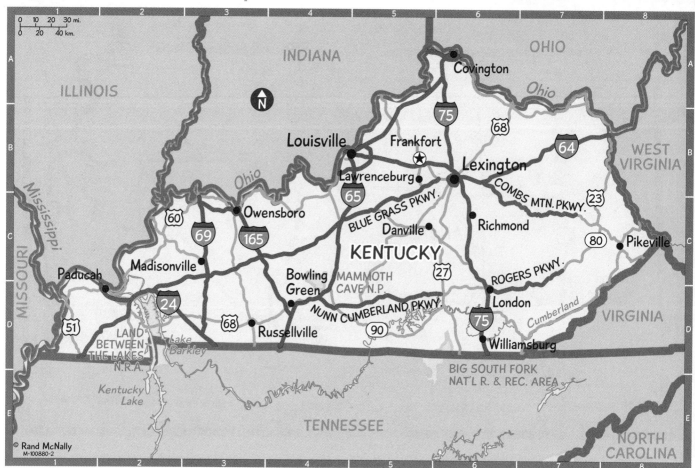

BOY Oh BOY!

The name "Ken" can be found in the first three letters of Kentucky. How many boys' names can you find hidden in the cities on the map of Kentucky?

Hint: All of the names do not occur at the beginning of the city names.

B-4
B-5
B-5
B-6
C-3
C-5
C-6
C-8
D-3
D-4
D-6
D-6

LouisiAna

Bald cypress	Magnolia	Eastern brown pelican

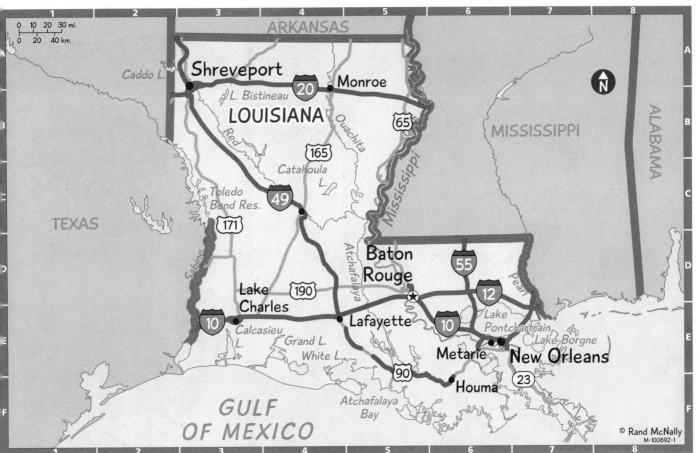

Map labels:
ARKANSAS
Caddo L.
Shreveport
L. Bistineau
Monroe
20
LOUISIANA
Red
Ouachita
65
165
Catahoula L.
Toledo Bend Res.
49
TEXAS
171
Sabine
Mississippi
Atchafalaya
MISSISSIPPI
ALABAMA
Baton Rouge
55
Pearl
12
Lake Charles
190
Calcasieu L.
Grand L.
White L.
Lafayette
10
Lake Pontchartrain
Lake Borgne
Metarie
New Orleans
90
Houma
23
GULF OF MEXICO
Atchafalaya Bay
N
© Rand McNally
M-100892-1

Big Rivers

Can you fit the names of these Louisiana rivers, bayous, and lakes into the grid? One of the lake names is in the puzzle to get you started.
Hint: Counting the number of letters in the words and using the color code will help.

RIVERS: Mississippi, Red, Ouachita, Sabine, Pearl, Atchafalaya, Black

BAYOUS: Teche, Lafourche, Macon, Boeuf, Dorcheat, D'Arbonne

LAKES: Pontchartrain, Calcasieu, White, Borgne, Caddo, Bistineau, Toledo Bend Reservoir, Grand, Catahoula

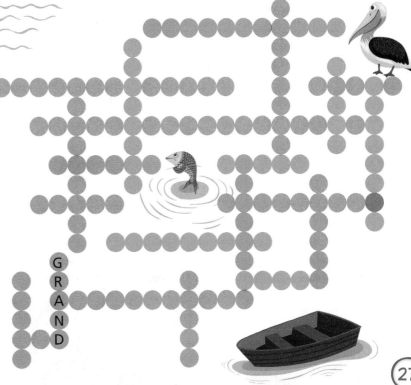

MainE

White pine | White pine cone & tassel | Chickadee

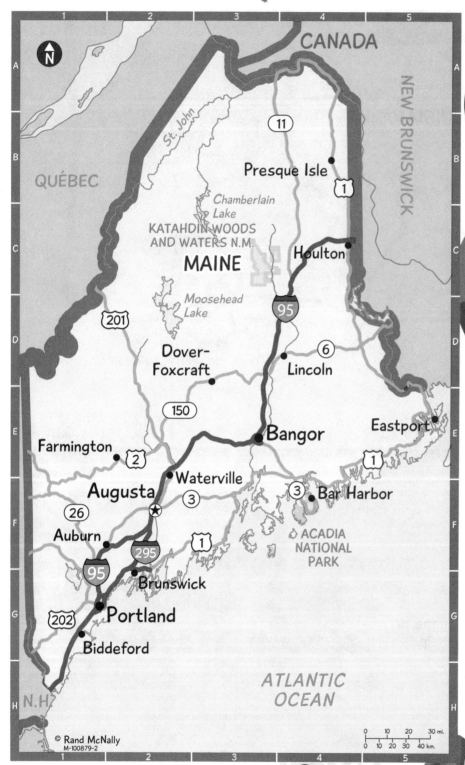

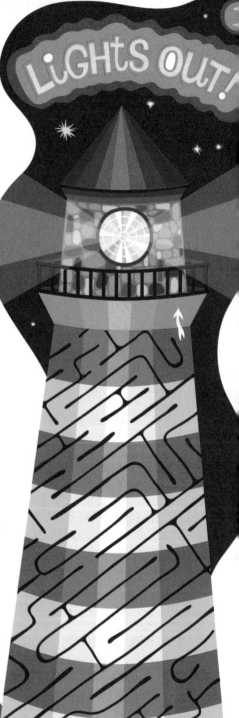

LiGHtS OUt!

Help the lighthouse keeper get to the top to warn the ships.

28

Nickname: The Old Line State | Capital: Annapolis

White oak | Black-eyed susan | Baltimore oriole

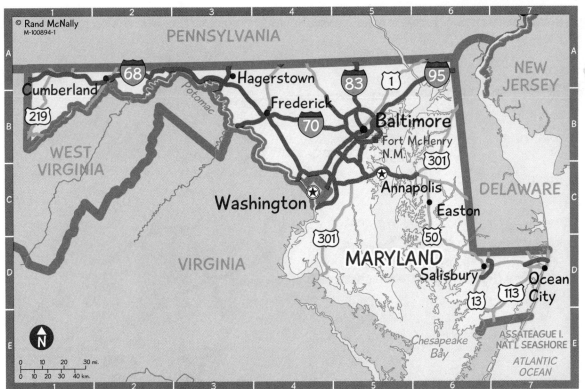

© Rand McNally
M-100894-1

PENNSYLVANIA

Cumberland
Hagerstown
Frederick
Baltimore
Fort McHenry N.M.
NEW JERSEY
WEST VIRGINIA
Washington
Annapolis
Easton
DELAWARE
VIRGINIA
MARYLAND
Salisbury
Ocean City
ASSATEAGUE I. NAT'L SEASHORE
Chesapeake Bay
ATLANTIC OCEAN

1. Oh! Say can you see, by the dawn's early light,
2. what so proudly we hailed at the twilight's last gleaming?
3. Whose broad stripes and bright stars through the perilous fight,
4. o'er the ramparts we watched were so gallantly streaming?
5. And the rockets' red glare,
6. the bombs bursting in air
7. gave proof through the night
8. that our flag was still there.
9. Oh! Say does that star-spangled banner yet wave
10. o'er the land of the free and the home of the brave?

Use the example at the right to understand the code. The letter G is in line number 1, word number 10, and letter number 3.

G	
line	1
word	10
letter	3

FLaG SoNG

Francis Scott Key wrote the National Anthem in Maryland during the Battle of Baltimore in the War of 1812. Solve the code to find out where he was when he wrote these famous words.

9	7	8	2	3	5	2	4	4	2	4	7	5	5
1	4	4	1	6	1	3	3	9	8	1	5	5	4
2	3	1	3	1	1	1	1	1	7	9	1	1	5	1

10	10	8	6	1	3	4	6	9	7	2	3	4	7
9	3	3	2	9	3	3	4	2	3	2	10	9	2
2	3	3	1	3	4	7	1	1	2	1	4	7	1

(29)

American elm | Mayflower | Black-capped chickadee

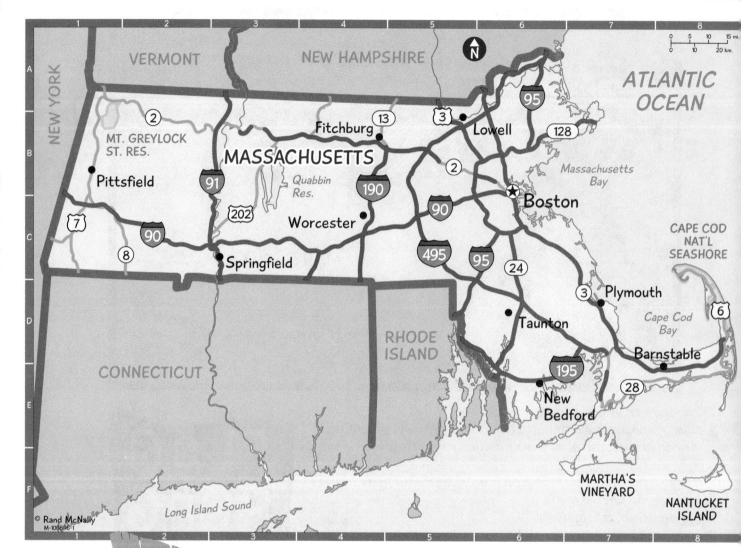

Bay Staters

Many famous people were born in or lived in Massachusetts. The names of fifteen of them are hidden in the word search on the next page. (Only the last names are hidden.)

(JOHN) ADAMS

(LOUISA MAY) ALCOTT

(SUSAN B.) ANTHONY

(CLARA) BARTON

(EMILY) DICKINSON

(W.E.B.) DUBOIS

(RALPH WALDO) EMERSON

(BENJAMIN) FRANKLIN

(JOHN) HANCOCK

(OLIVER WENDELL) HOLMES

(WINSLOW) HOMER

(JOHN F.) KENNEDY

(EDGAR ALLAN) POE

(PAUL) REVERE

(NORMAN) ROCKWELL

A D R L P O E
E X I H O L M E S
F A N C D E C E R E
G R R K A H M K R A
M B A I R E E E W H
L S L N R E V H A E N
K E I S K E M N N O L A
N E O O R L C O T R L L
N N N B O I R H C Y
D N C U A N O A
V K E B D T N I D
T H O D T R Y E A
A D A M S Y U

MIchigan

White pine | Apple blossom | Robin

You are the inspector for this line of new cars in Detroit, the "Motor City." Circle the six differences between the standard and the other cars.

MINN.

ISLE ROYALE N.P.

Copper Harbor

LAKE SUPERIOR

CANADA

ONTARIO

PICTURED ROCKS NAT'L LAKESHORE

Ironwood

Marquette

2

141

Sault Ste. Marie

75

Iron Mtn.

2

Mackinaw City

WIS.

Escanaba

SLEEPING BEAR SAND DUNES NAT'L LAKESHORE

Alpena

Menominee

Traverse City

MICHIGAN

23

LAKE HURON

31

Ludington

10

75

Bay City

131

127

Saginaw

Port Huron

Muskegon

Grand Rapids

Flint

69

LAKE MICHIGAN

Lansing

96

St. Joseph

94

Detroit

LAKE ERIE

INDIANA

OHIO

© Rand McNally
M-100870-1

Standard

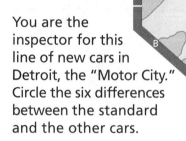

QUaLitY Control

(32)

MiNnesota

Nickname: The North Star State

Capital: St. Paul

Norway pine | Pink-and-white lady's slipper | Common loon

MANITOBA
CANADA
ONTARIO
Lake of the Woods
International Falls
Upper Red Lake
VOYAGEURS N.P.
Vermilion L.
71
53
Lower Red Lake
Lake Winnibigoshish
NORTH DAKOTA
Bemidji
L. Itasca
Leech Lake
Moorhead
MINNESOTA
Duluth
LAKE SUPERIOR
61
35
Mille Lacs L.
94
St. Cloud
WISCONSIN
Red
12
SOUTH DAKOTA
75
71
Minneapolis
St. Paul
Mississippi
14
Mankato
52
61
Rochester
90
90
IOWA
Rand McNally
M-100896-2
0 10 20 30 mi.
0 20 40 km.

Lots a Lakes

Minnesota is called the land of 10,000 lakes. Use the coordinates and clues to find a few of these lakes.

ACROSS
3. E–3; unscramble **LIMEL SCAL**
4. C–4; rhymes with 1,000,000
6. D–3; hope not to find these in the lake

DOWN
1. C–2; above and rosy
2. D–3; 14 letters in this name
5. D–2; L. and unscramble **ASTICA**

MiSsissippi

Nickname: The Magnolia State

Capital: Jackson

Magnolia | Magnolia | Mockingbird

TENNESSEE

ARKANSAS

© Rand McNally
M-100897-2

Corinth
72
55
22
45
278
Tupelo
Clarksdale
MISSISSIPPI
82
Columbus
82
Greenville
Winona
25
45
61
49
Jackson
Meridian
20
Vicksburg
55
Pearl
84
Natchez
98
Hattiesburg
61
98
59
49
63
LOUISIANA
Biloxi
10
Gulfport
GULF ISLANDS
NAT'L SEASHORE
GULF OF MEXICO

ALABAMA

Mississippi

PLENTY OF P's

Can you find 20 things that start with "P" in this scene on the Mississippi River?

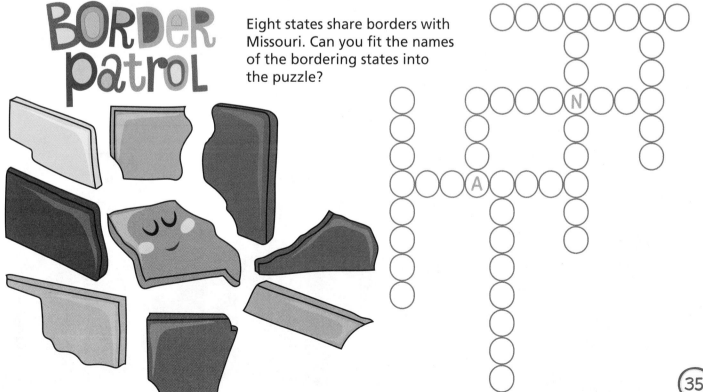

BORDER patrol

Eight states share borders with Missouri. Can you fit the names of the bordering states into the puzzle?

MonTana

Nickname: The Treasure State **Capital:** Helena

Ponderosa pine | Bitterroot | Western meadowlark

After a morning of boarding at Big Sky Resort, this snowboarder went in for lunch. When he came out, he couldn't remember where he had put his snowboard. Using the clues that he recalls, help him find his board.

SNOWBOARD SHUFFLE

1. His snowboard isn't next to a pair of skis.
2. His snowboard is not blue.
3. His snowboard is next to a blue snowboard.

NEbraska

The Cornhusker State

Capital:
Lincoln

Cottonwood | Goldenrod | Western meadowlark

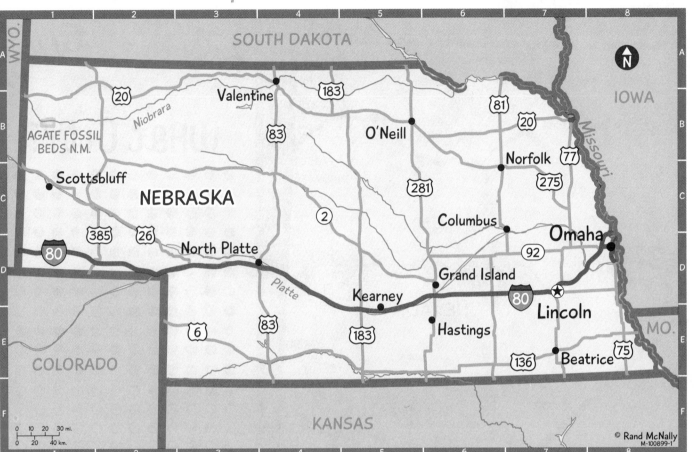

thrown for a loop

The cowboy tradition is alive and kicking in Nebraska. Here, a few cowboys have been practicing their roping tricks. Some of the ropes will form knots when both ends are pulled. Can you tell which ones?

NeVada

Nickname: The Silver State | **Capital:** Carson City

Single-leaf piñon | Sagebrush | Mountain bluebird

OREGON
IDAHO

A

McDermitt

140 95

93

223

UTAH

B

Winnemucca

Elko

80

West Wendover

Spring Creek

Pyramid Lake

80

305

C

278

Sparks

Fallon

50

50

Reno

Ely

D

Carson City

NEVADA

GREAT BASIN N.P.

Lake Tahoe

95

376

6

93

E

Tonopah

BASIN AND RANGE N.M.

CALIFORNIA

DEATH VALLEY N.P.

Mesquite

F

15

95

LAKE MEAD N.R.A.

G

Las Vegas

ARIZONA

Henderson

95

Colorado

H

N

© Rand McNally
M-100900-2

0 10 20 30 mi.
0 20 40 km.

BRiGHt LiGHtS, WHat CitY?

Hidden within the colorful lights is the answer to the question. All you have to do is fill in the bulbs marked with an "X."

What city has the highest electric bills in America?

38

New Hampshire

Nickname: The Granite State **Capital:** Concord

White birch | Purple lilac | Purple finch

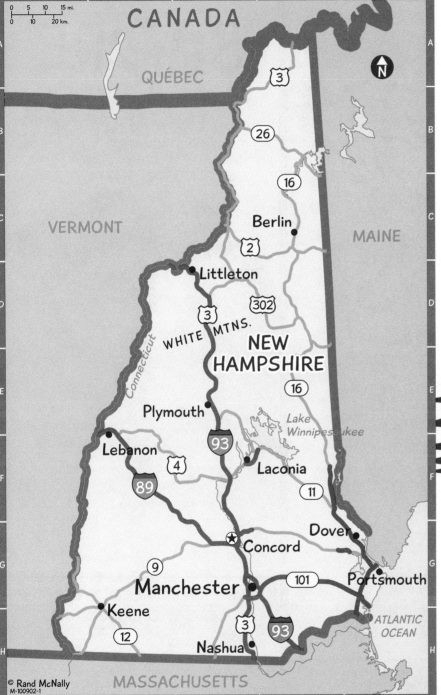

CANADA

QUÉBEC

VERMONT

MAINE

Berlin

Littleton

WHITE MTNS.

NEW HAMPSHIRE

Plymouth

Lebanon

Laconia

Lake Winnipesaukee

Dover

Concord

Manchester

Keene

Portsmouth

ATLANTIC OCEAN

Nashua

MASSACHUSETTS

© Rand McNally
M-100902-1

Connecticut

UNDER a SPELL

How many things can you find in this scene that can only be spelled using letters found in the words NEW HAMPSHIRE?

New Jersey

Red oak | Purple violet | Eastern goldfinch

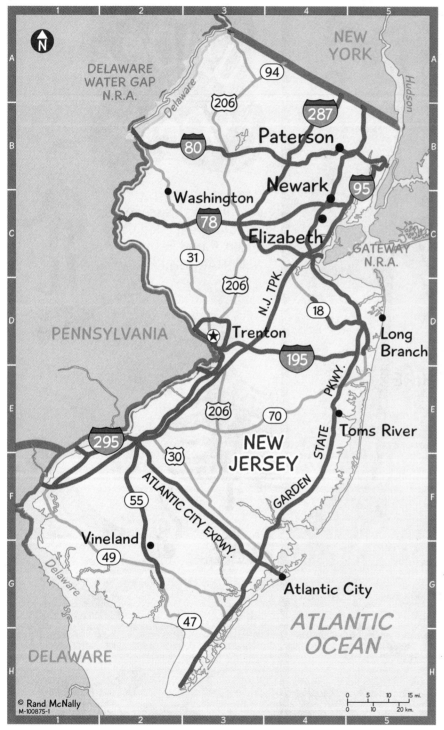

NEW YORK

DELAWARE WATER GAP N.R.A.

94
206
287
Paterson
80
Newark
95
Washington
78
Elizabeth
GATEWAY N.R.A.
31
206
N.J. TPK.
18
Trenton
Long Branch
195
206
70
Toms River
NEW JERSEY
30
GARDEN STATE PKWY.
55
ATLANTIC CITY EXPWY.
295
Vineland
49
Atlantic City
47
ATLANTIC OCEAN

PENNSYLVANIA
DELAWARE
Hudson
Delaware

© Rand McNally
M-100875-1

0 5 10 15 mi.
0 10 20 km.

SHORE THINGS

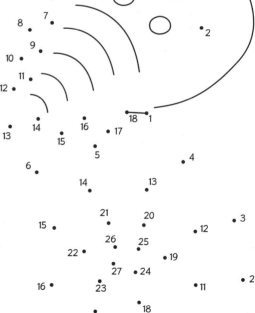

Connect the dots to see what's on this New Jersey beach.

New Mexico

Nickname: Land of Enchantment

Capital: Santa Fe

Piñon pine | Yucca | Roadrunner

© Rand McNally
M-100903-2

COLORADO

UTAH
ARIZONA

N

RÍO GRANDE DEL NORTE N.M.

Raton

Farmington
491

84 Taos
64

Santa Fe
25

Los Alamos
CHACO CULTURE N.H.P.

Las Vegas
54

Gallup
40
550

Albuquerque
40

EL MALPAIS N.M.

Clovis

60
60

NEW MEXICO

70

Socorro

Roswell

Pecos
Rio Grande

54
380

180

Silver City
25

WHITE SANDS N.P.

Alamogordo
285

Carlsbad

ORGAN MTNS DESERT PEAKS N.M.
70
10

Las Cruces

CARLSBAD CAVERNS N.P.

TEXAS

MEXICO
CHIHUAHUA

0 10 20 30 mi.
0 20 40 km.

The Hot Air Balloon Festival in Albuquerque is the most photographed event of its kind in the world! New Mexico is famous for another hot thing—its Southwestern food. Can you find the 10 chili peppers hiding in this scene?

HOT tiME

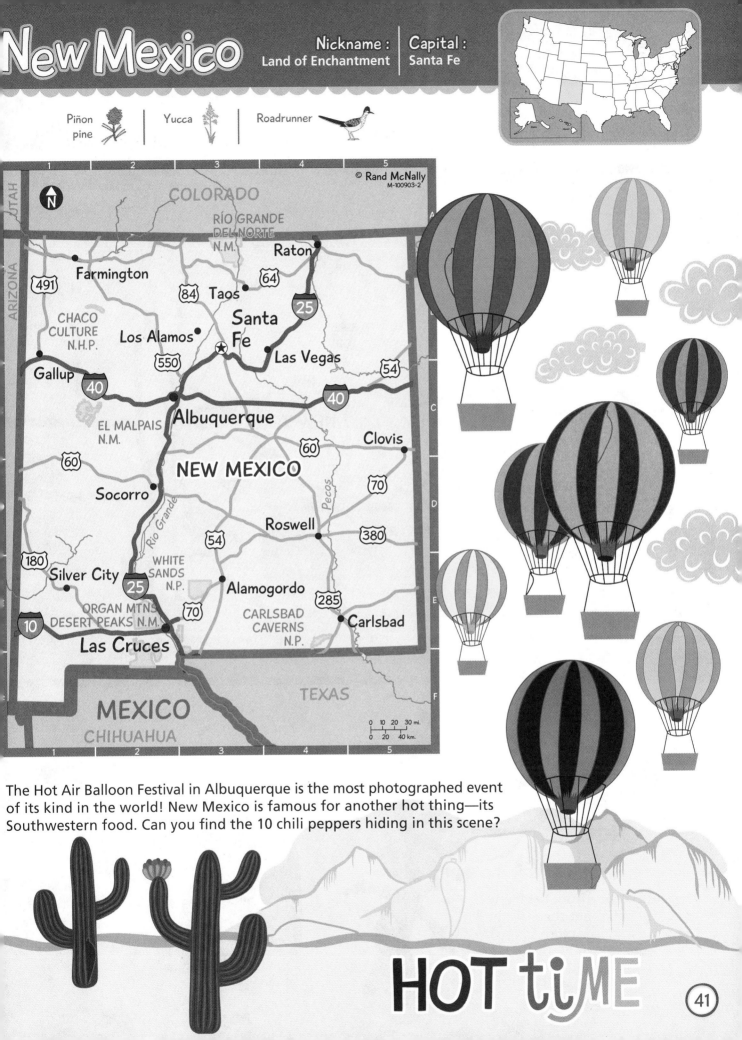

New York

Sugar maple | Rose | Red-breasted bluebird

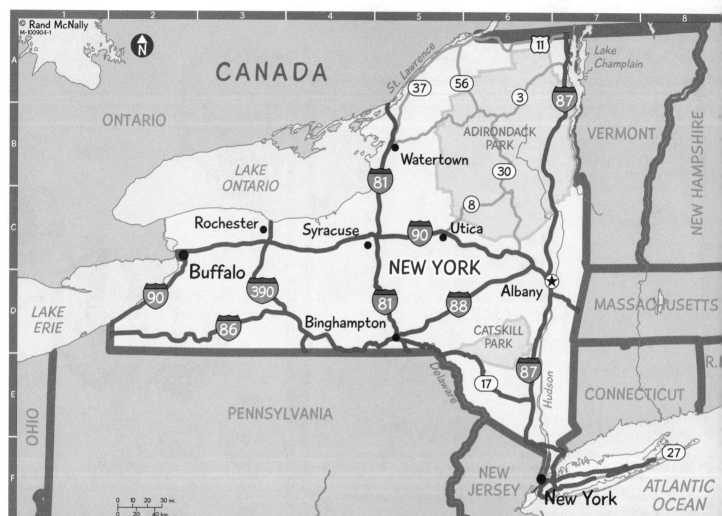

PROBLEMS at the PARK

The state of New York has many beautiful parks, but there seems to be something strange going on in this one. Can you spot 10 things wrong in the park?

North Carolina

Nickname: The Tar Heel State | **Capital:** Raleigh

Pine | Dogwood | Cardinal

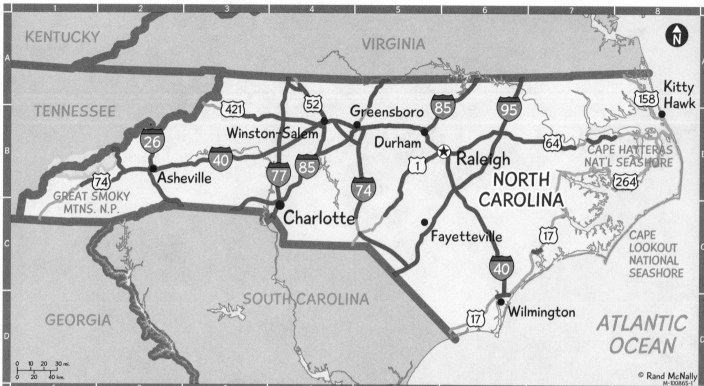

First in Flight

4

The beach community of Kitty Hawk (B-8) was the site of the Wright brothers' first airplane flight. Try to find 26 things that start with "F" in this beach scene.

American elm | Wild prairie rose | Western meadowlark

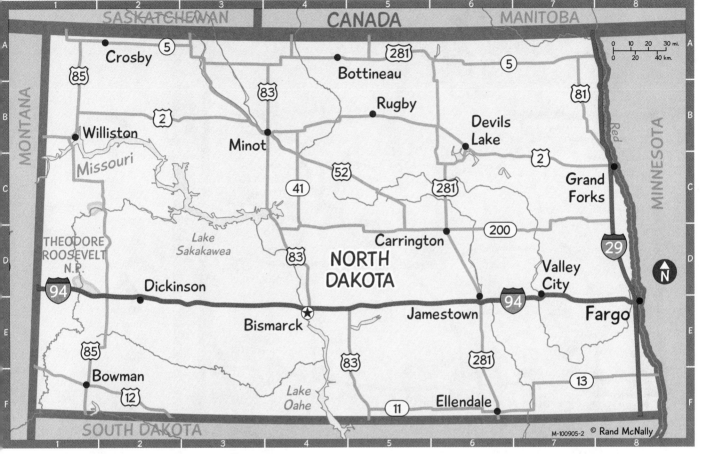

SASKATCHEWAN | CANADA | MANITOBA

Crosby
85
281
5
Bottineau
83
Rugby
81
Williston
2
Devils Lake
Minot
Missouri
52
2
41
Grand Forks
Red
MONTANA
MINNESOTA
THEODORE ROOSEVELT N.P.
Lake Sakakawea
Carrington
200
NORTH DAKOTA
83
281
29
Valley City
94
Dickinson
N
Bismarck
Jamestown
94
Fargo
85
83
281
13
Bowman
12
Lake Oahe
11
Ellendale

SOUTH DAKOTA

M-100905-2 © Rand McNally

Secret Cities

Figure out the names of six North Dakota cities using the word puzzles below.

1)  + =

_____

4) + =

_____

2) GRRR + and + =

_____

5) + - C + L =

_____

3) V + + =

_____

6) + ing + =

_____

(45)

OHio

Nickname :
The Buckeye State

Capital :
Columbus

Buckeye | Scarlet carnation | Cardinal

SpLit Cities

The names of many cities in Ohio can be split into two smaller words. For example, DAY and TON go together to form DAYTON. Match the words in column A with the words in column B to spell 12 Ohio cities. All of the cities are listed on the map.

46

Column A	Column B
FIND	LAND
NEW	MOUTH
ASH	FIELD
CAN	TOWN
WHITE	ARK
SPRING	TON
LOG	BORN
AT	AN
PORTS	FORD
OX	LAY
FAIR	HALL
MIDDLE	HENS

Redbud | Mistletoe | Scissor-tailed flycatcher

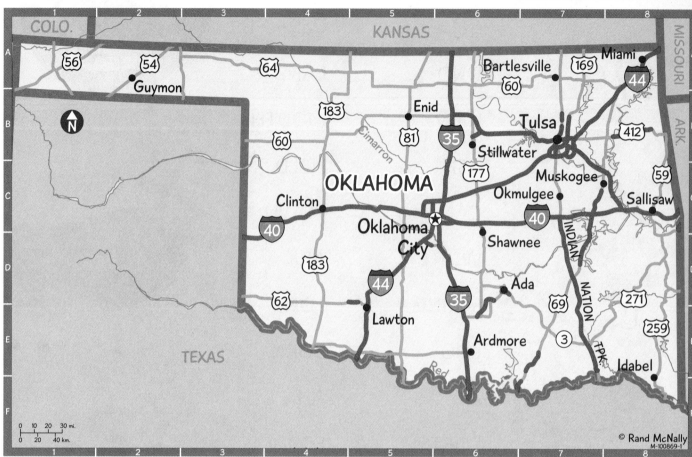

Scrambled Cities

Unscramble the names of these Oklahoma towns and you'll be OK!

DINE (B-5) _____

BILEAD (E-8) _____

LOWTAN (E-5) _____

WLASSAIL (C-8) _____

LEEKOMUG (C-7) _____

MOUNGY (A-2) _____

USALT (B-7) _____

AMIMI (A-8) _____

SHEENWA (C-6) _____

TALLIWERTS (B-6) _____

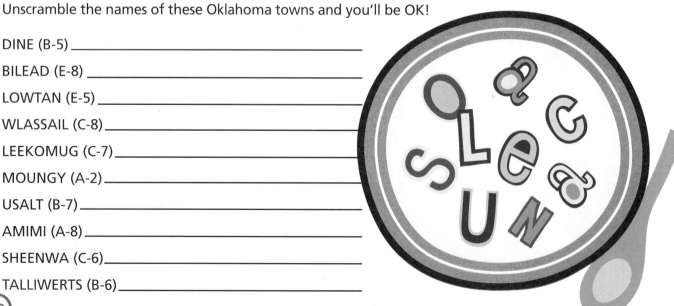

OREgon

Douglas fir | Oregon grape | Western meadowlark

© Rand McNally
M-100883-1

WASHINGTON

PACIFIC OCEAN

Astoria — 30
26
101
84
Portland
Salem
22
20
Corvallis
126
Eugene
58
5
Coos Bay
Roseburg
CAPE BLANCO
101
Medford
97
CASCADE SISKIYOU N.M.
Klamath Falls
140

OREGON DUNES N.R.A.

RANGE
CASCADE

The Dalles
26
97
Pendleton
11
395
La Grande
84
Snake
IDAHO

HELLS CANYON N.R.A.

John Day
26
OREGON
20
Ontario
31
CRATER LAKE N.P.
Upper Klamath Lake
395
Malheur Lake
Harney Lake
78
Burns Junction
95

Columbia

N

0 10 20 30 mi.
0 20 40 km.

CALIFORNIA | NEVADA

Dive In

These two tide pools on the Oregon coast are almost exactly alike. Can you spot the nine differences between them?

PennsylvAnia

Nickname: The Keystone State | **Capital:** Harrisburg

Hemlock | Mountain laurel | Ruffed grouse

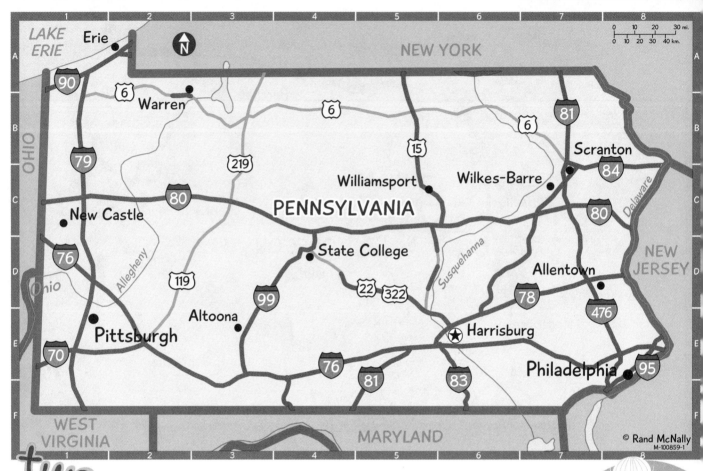

LAKE ERIE
Erie
90
6
Warren
OHIO
79
80
New Castle
PENNSYLVANIA
Williamsport
Wilkes-Barre
Scranton
84
6
6
81
15
NEW YORK
219
76
119
Allegheny
Ohio
State College
99
22 322
Susquehanna
Allentown
78
476
80
Delaware
NEW JERSEY
Altoona
Pittsburgh
70
76
81
83
Harrisburg
Philadelphia
95
WEST VIRGINIA
MARYLAND
© Rand McNally
M-100859-1

two of a kind

Two of the squares in this Pennsylvania Dutch quilt are exactly the same. Can you find them?

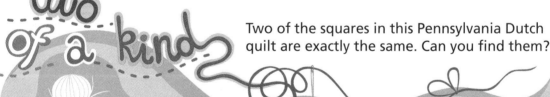

50

Rhode Island

Red maple | Violet | Rhode Island red

in the RED

People in Rhode Island must like the color red. Their state bird is the Rhode Island red and their state tree is the red maple. Use the clues below to identify words that have RED in them.

1. Stop signal_____

2. Tall California tree_____

3. Colors of the U.S. flag_____

4. Become very angry_____

5. Story about a girl, her grandmother, and a wolf
_____

6. Walking surface for movie stars_____

7. Carrot top_____

WELCOME to RHODE iSLAND

South Carolina

Nickname : The Palmetto State | Capital : Columbia

Palmetto | Carolina jessamine | Carolina wren

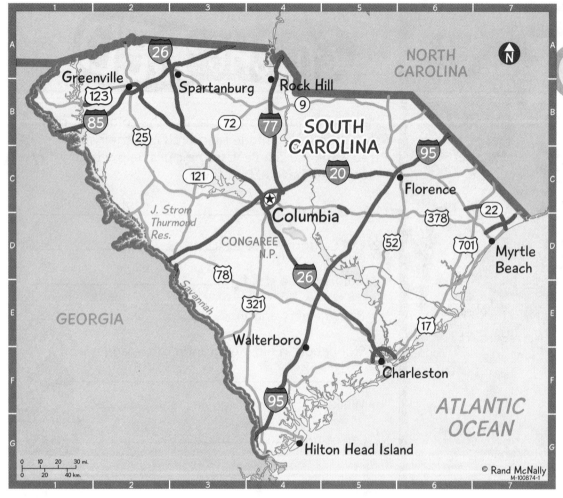

Cotton Critters

Cotton is an important crop in South Carolina. Can you find the pesky boll weevils hidden in the cotton plants? Circle them before they damage the cotton.

52

South Dakota

Nickname: The Mount Rushmore State

Capital: Pierre

Black Hills spruce | Pasque flower | Chinese ring-necked pheasant

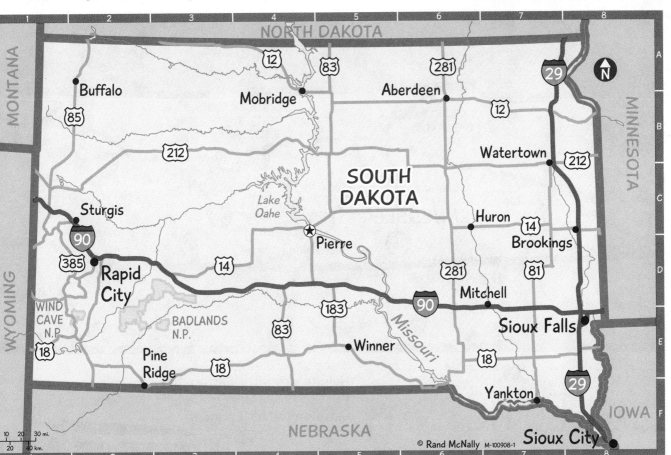

MONTANA

NORTH DAKOTA

Buffalo

85

Mobridge

12

83

281

Aberdeen

29

N

212

12

Watertown

212

SOUTH DAKOTA

Lake Oahe

Sturgis

90

385

Pierre

14

Huron

14

Brookings

281

81

Rapid City

WIND CAVE N.P.

BADLANDS N.P.

14

183

83

90

Mitchell

Sioux Falls

Winner

Missouri

18

WYOMING

18

Pine Ridge

18

Yankton

29

IOWA

NEBRASKA

Sioux City

0 10 20 30 mi.
0 20 40 km.

© Rand McNally M-100908-1

MINNESOTA

The pictures below show the steps in making a sweater—starting with shearing a sheep for wool. However, the pictures are not in the right order. If you write the letters in the corner of the pictures in the order in which they should be placed, the letters will complete a fact about South Dakota.

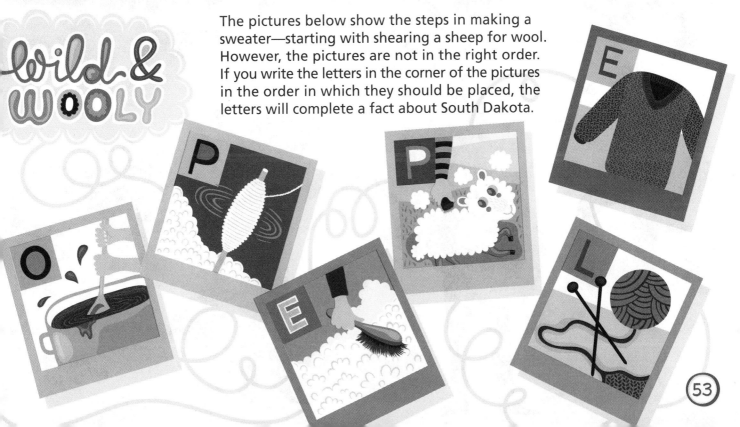

wild & wooly

53

TeNNessee

Tulip tree | Iris | Mockingbird

Help this country western band make it to the Grand Ole Opry on time in the maze on the next page.

The Road is Closed.

ROAD CLOSED

© Rand McNally
M-100868-1

54

ROAD CLOSED

STOP

GRAND OLE OPRY

TeXas

Nickname: **The Lone Star State** | Capital: **Austin**

Pecan | Bluebonnet | Mockingbird

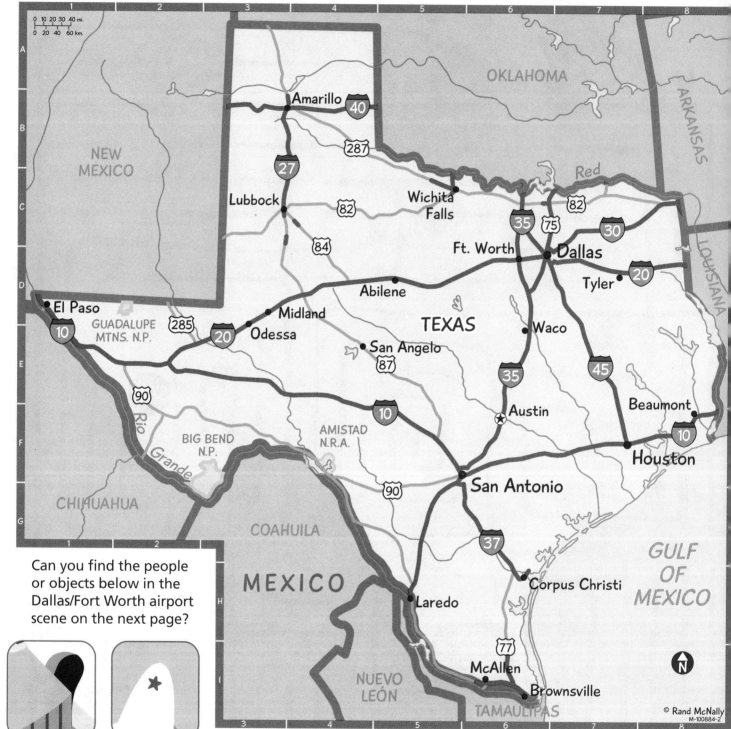

OKLAHOMA

NEW MEXICO

Amarillo **40**

287

27

Lubbock

82

Wichita Falls

84

Red

82

35 **75**

30

Ft. Worth

Dallas

Tyler **20**

LOUISIANA

Abilene

TEXAS

El Paso

10

GUADALUPE MTNS. N.P.

285

Midland

Odessa

20

San Angelo

87

Waco

35

45

Beaumont

Austin

10

90

Rio Grande

BIG BEND N.P.

AMISTAD N.R.A.

10

Houston

CHIHUAHUA

90

San Antonio

GULF OF MEXICO

COAHUILA

37

MEXICO

Corpus Christi

Laredo

NUEVO LEÓN

77

McAllen

Brownsville

TAMAULIPAS

© Rand McNally
M-100884-2

N

Can you find the people or objects below in the Dallas/Fort Worth airport scene on the next page?

56

UTah

Blue spruce | Sego lily | American seagull

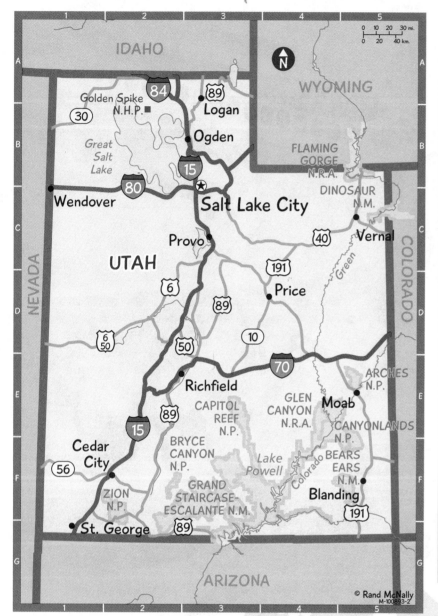

Utah is home to many National Parks and Monuments. Circle the names, listed below the map, in the puzzle.

T	G	R	P	P	H	B	L	S	T	I	Y	B
T	L	I	V	E	S	A	R	C	H	E	S	E
A	E	B	A	B	R	E	Z	Q	R	O	M	A
E	N	N	Q	P	D	I	N	O	S	A	U	R
G	C	O	U	L	E	N	N	B	K	I	R	S
R	A	O	C	I	F	G	S	G	N	T	A	E
O	N	T	A	O	E	X	D	O	Z	B	D	A
G	Y	F	I	K	G	G	I	L	L	I	B	R
G	O	G	B	E	C	W	N	D	A	W	O	S
N	N	K	P	N	P	S	H	E	C	V	Y	N
I	S	T	I	R	D	O	U	N	H	R	R	D
M	D	A	D	T	E	N	D	S	B	O	C	R
A	T	E	J	C	V	P	L	P	A	I	H	A
L	X	R	E	O	Y	T	S	I	M	Z	S	I
F	O	R	S	K	B	R	A	K	N	S	P	V
C	A	P	I	T	O	L	R	E	E	F	G	S
M	G	I	L	K	B	I	I	J	R	I	A	O
A	Q	R	L	E	B	S	H	O	A	O	N	G
O	J	C	R	A	Y	A	D	C	L	N	W	H
C	A	N	Y	O	N	L	A	N	D	S	P	C
T	A	H	H	R	N	I	Z	L	A	W	M	I
R	C	A	L	E	X	S	Y	T	L	P	I	N
S	K	A	E	R	B	R	A	D	E	C	T	C

ARCHES   DINOSAUR

BEARS EARS   FLAMING GORGE

CANYONLANDS   GLEN CANYON

CAPITOL REEF   GOLDEN SPIKE

CEDAR BREAKS   ZION

Vermont

Sugar maple | Red clover | Hermit thrush

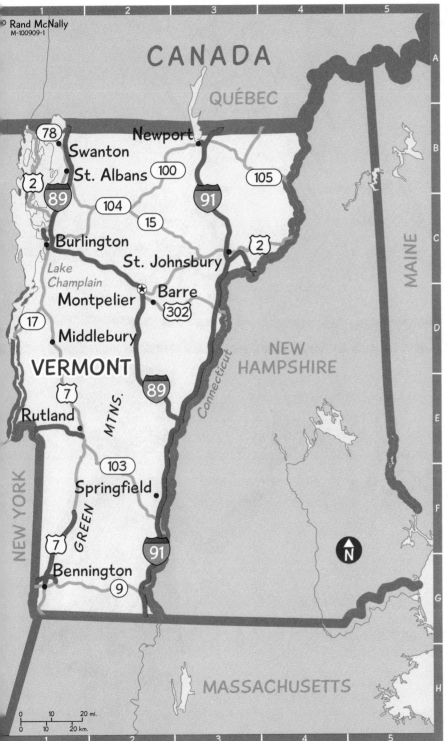

© Rand McNally
M-100909-1

CANADA

QUÉBEC

78 Newport
Swanton
St. Albans 100   105
2
89
104
15
Burlington
St. Johnsbury 2
Lake Champlain
Montpelier ★ Barre
302
17
Middlebury
VERMONT
7
Rutland
MTNS.
103
Springfield
GREEN
7
91
Bennington
9

MAINE

NEW HAMPSHIRE

Connecticut

89

91

N

NEW YORK

MASSACHUSETTS

0 10 20 mi.
0 10 20 km.

All of the facts about Vermont below are true...except for one. To find out which one is not true, solve the equation. The value of X will equal the number next to the false statement.

1. Native Americans taught Europeans how to tap maple trees for syrup.

2. Only Wyoming has fewer residents than Vermont.

3. Vermont was once its own country, with its own money!

4. Grandma Moses, a Vermont painter, worked until she was 101 years old.

5. Ice cream from Vermont is popular because cows there have a higher cream content in their milk.

X = The number of the false fact
X = A - B + C
A = B + 4
B = C + 2
C = 1

UNBELIEVABLE!

VirginiA

Dogwood | Dogwood | Cardinal

COLONIAL CLUES

This Virginia city was the center of politics and culture in colonial times. Use the clues to find out the name of this city.

1. It's about 50 miles southeast of Richmond.

2. It's about 35 miles northwest of Norfolk.

3. It's at coordinate C-7.

The city is _____

Nickname : The Evergreen State | **Capital :** Olympia

Western hemlock  | Coast rhododendron  | Willow goldfinch

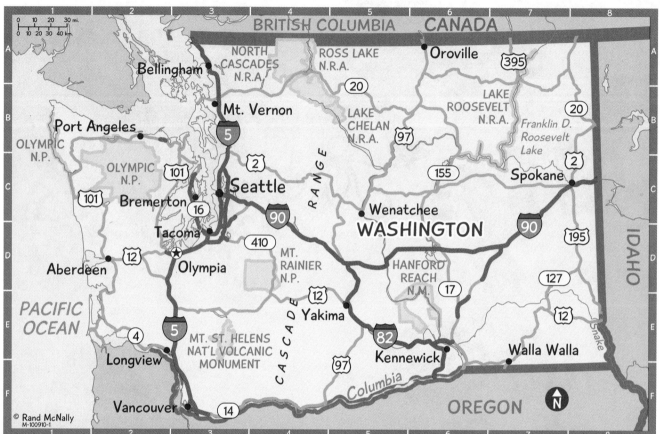

In the spaces provided, write the **last** letters of the objects shown in the boxes. When you're finished, the letters will spell out the name of an event that was started in 1909 by Sonora Louise Smart Dodd in Spokane, Washington.

___ ___ ___ ___ ___ ___ ___ ,

___ ___ ___

West Virginia

Sugar maple | Rhododendron | Cardinal

Map

- Weirton
- Wheeling
- OHIO
- PENNSYLVANIA
- Ohio
- Morgantown
- 68
- MARYLAND
- Parkersburg
- Clarksburg
- Martinsburg
- Harpers Ferry
- 50
- Potomac
- Weston
- 33
- 219
- WEST VIRGINIA
- 77
- 79
- 64
- Huntington
- Charleston
- NEW RIVER GORGE NAT'L PARK
- APPALACHIAN MTNS.
- New
- 19
- 119
- Beckley
- 64
- VIRGINIA
- KENTUCKY
- Tug Fork
- 77
- 219

© Rand McNally
M-100911-2

Falling Leaves

Cross out and unscramble the words that answer the clues. An interesting fact about West Virigina will be left when you're finished.

Clues

1. The town that is furthest north
2. The river that makes up most of the west border
3. The town that is "NOT SEW" scrambled
4. The river that begins with a "P"
5. The town that is the farthest east
6. The river that makes up part of the southwestern border
7. The state that borders West Virginia to the southwest
8. The state capital

TUG FORK
HARPERS FERRY
AMERICA'S
NEW
CHARLESTON
WEIRTON
RIVER
KENTUCKY
WESTON
THE
RIVER
IS
OHIO
POTOMAC
OLDEST

63

WIsconsin

Nickname: The Badger State | **Capital:** Madison

Sugar maple | Wood violet | Robin

CANADA

Lake Superior

MINNESOTA

APOSTLE ISLANDS NAT'L LAKESHORE

Superior

Ashland

53

63

51

MICHIGAN

45

8

Rice Lake

WISCONSIN

141

94

Wausau

Eau Claire

10

53

10

Green Bay

42

La Crosse

39

Oshkosh

90

Mississippi

Wisconsin

43

Baraboo

41

61

Madison

94

Milwaukee

18

90

43

Racine

IOWA

ILLINOIS

Lake Michigan

© Rand McNally
M-100912-2

Clowning around

In 1884, five brothers held their first circus with farm animals and jugglers in Wisconsin. Over time, it became the world-famous Ringling Brothers Circus. Find out what town held that first event and now has the Circus World Museum. Solve the puzzle below and read the one-letter answers from top to bottom.

1. A letter in BEAR, but not in TRAPEZE. _____

2. A letter in LAKE and MICHIGAN. _____

3. A letter in SPARTA and MERRILL. _____

4. A letter in SUGAR and MAPLE. _____

5. A letter in BRIE, but not in AMERICAN. _____

6. A letter in HOLSTEIN and COW. _____

7. A letter in TRACTOR, but not in CART. _____

64

WYoming

Cottonwood

Rhododendron

Western meadowlark

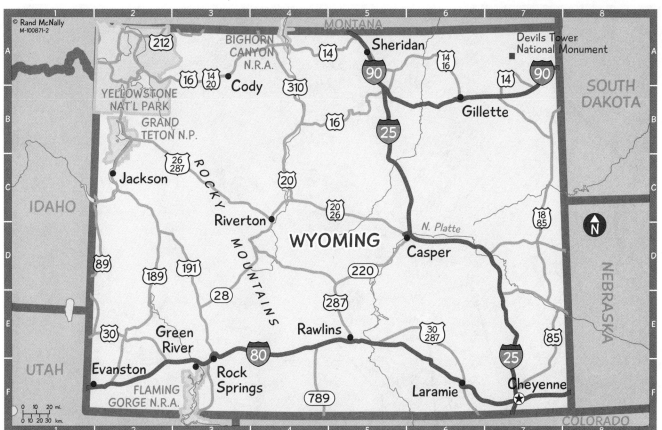

Climb to the top! Start at the bottom left and see if you can make it to the top of Devils Tower (A-7).

Canada | Capital : Ottawa

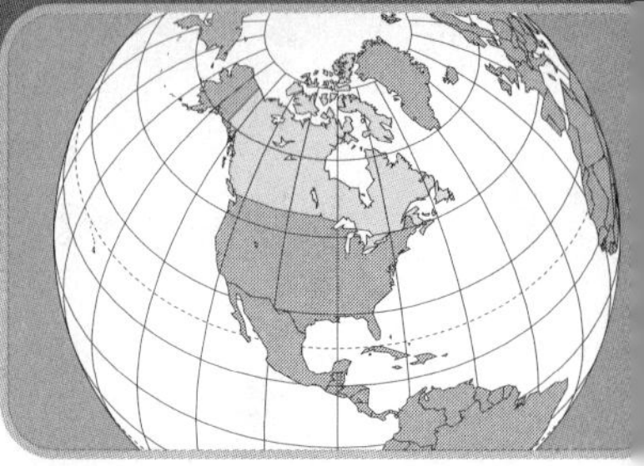

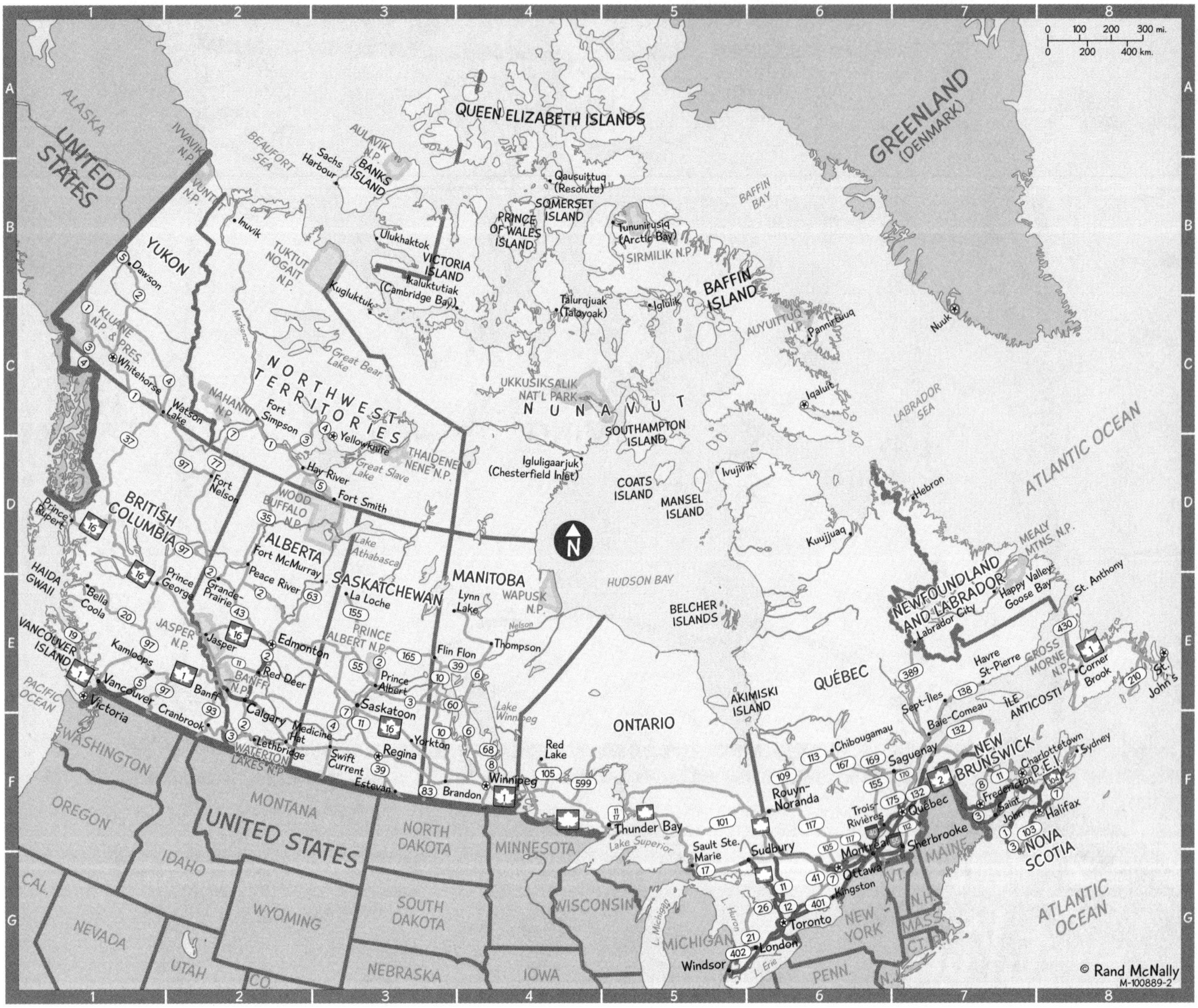

QUEEN ELIZABETH ISLANDS
GREENLAND (DENMARK)
BAFFIN BAY
BEAUFORT SEA
ALASKA
UNITED STATES
YUKON
NORTHWEST TERRITORIES
NUNAVUT
BRITISH COLUMBIA
ALBERTA
SASKATCHEWAN
MANITOBA
ONTARIO
QUÉBEC
NEWFOUNDLAND AND LABRADOR
NEW BRUNSWICK
NOVA SCOTIA
P.E.I.
BANKS ISLAND
VICTORIA ISLAND
PRINCE OF WALES ISLAND
SOMERSET ISLAND
BAFFIN ISLAND
SOUTHAMPTON ISLAND
COATS ISLAND
MANSEL ISLAND
BELCHER ISLANDS
AKIMISKI ISLAND
HAIDA GWAII
VANCOUVER ISLAND
HUDSON BAY
LABRADOR SEA
ATLANTIC OCEAN
PACIFIC OCEAN
Qausuittuq (Resolute)
Tununirusiq (Arctic Bay)
Ikaluktutiak (Cambridge Bay)
Talurqjuak (Taloyoak)
Igluligaarjuk (Chesterfield Inlet)
Iqaluit
Nuuk
Inuvik
Dawson
Whitehorse
Yellowknife
Fort Simpson
Hay River
Fort Smith
Prince Rupert
Prince George
Fort McMurray
Edmonton
Jasper
Kamloops
Vancouver
Victoria
Banff
Calgary
Red Deer
Lethbridge
Medicine Hat
Saskatoon
Regina
Prince Albert
Brandon
Winnipeg
Flin Flon
Thompson
Thunder Bay
Sault Ste. Marie
Sudbury
Toronto
Ottawa
Kingston
London
Windsor
Montréal
Québec
Trois-Rivières
Sherbrooke
Saguenay
Chibougamau
Rouyn-Noranda
Sept-Îles
Baie-Comeau
Labrador City
Happy Valley-Goose Bay
St. Anthony
Corner Brook
St. John's
Fredericton
Saint John
Charlottetown
Halifax
Sydney
WASHINGTON
OREGON
IDAHO
MONTANA
WYOMING
NORTH DAKOTA
SOUTH DAKOTA
MINNESOTA
WISCONSIN
MICHIGAN
IOWA
NEBRASKA
NEW YORK
PENN.
MAINE
Lake Superior
© Rand McNally
M-100889-2

Take a Gander!

Hey! That Canadian goose shouldn't be flying upside down! How many other mistakes can you find in the Canadian scene on the next page?

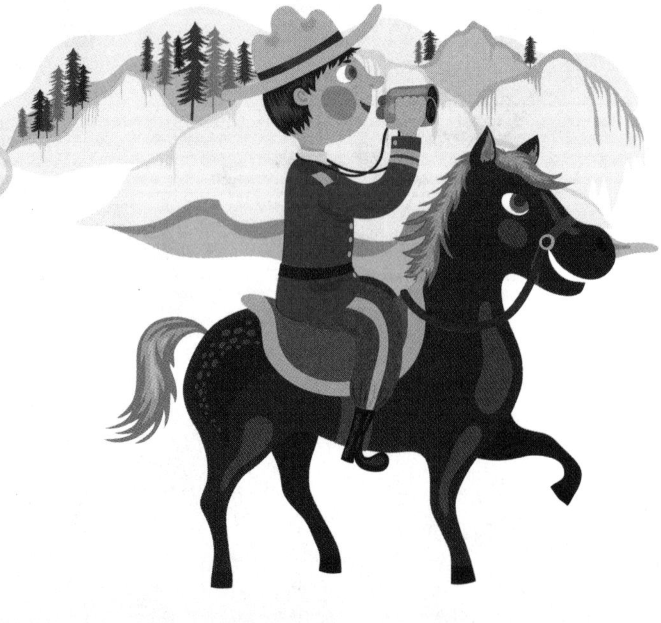

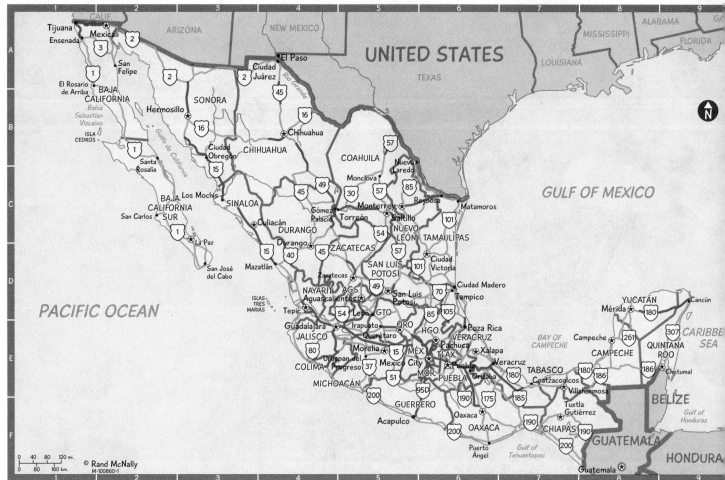

1. This body of water is to the east of Quintana Roo.

2. This city is in the northwest corner of the country.

3. This state on the south of the Bay of Campeche has the same name as a spicy sauce.

4. This food is a flat bread made from corn.

5. This river, or *rio*, forms much of the border between Mexico and the U.S.

6. This cliff-diving location is the southernmost point on highway 95D.

7. This city's name is a combination of Mexico and California.

8. This state in northern Mexico shares its name with a breed of dogs.

9. This body of water lies west of the Baja Peninsula.

10. This country lies east of Chiapas.

11. As you take highway 45 north, the last city you go through before leaving Mexico is _____.

12. This city is directly across the border to the north of question #11.

13. This country is south of Quintana Roo.

14. This "little beautiful" city is the capital city of the state of Sonora.

SOUTH OF the BORDER

Cross out the words in the puzzle that answer the questions on the opposite page. An interesting fact about Mexico will be left when you're finished. Read it from top to bottom.

MEXICANS

TORTILLA

as

CHIHUAHUA

PACIFIC OCEAN

TIJUANA
BELIZE
WERO
ACAPULCO
EL PASO
KNOWN
CIUDAD JUAREZ
the
men
MEXICALI
of
HERMOSILLO
TABASCO

RIO GRANDE

ONCE

CARIBBEAN SEA

GUATEMALA

CORN

License Plate Game

Keep an eye out for license plates from all over the United States.
Cross off the state when you see its plate.

Alabama	Hawaii	Massachusetts	New Mexico	South Dakota
Alaska	Idaho	Michigan	New York	Tennessee
Arizona	Illinois	Minnesota	North Carolina	Texas
Arkansas	Indiana	Mississippi	North Dakota	Utah
California	Iowa	Missouri	Ohio	Vermont
Colorado	Kansas	Montana	Oklahoma	Virginia
Connecticut	Kentucky	Nebraska	Oregon	Washington
Delaware	Louisiana	Nevada	Pennsylvania	West Virginia
Florida	Maine	New Hampshire	Rhode Island	Wisconsin
Georgia	Maryland	New Jersey	South Carolina	Wyoming

are we there yet?

Contents

Don't miss your flight

Hurry and find your seat before the plane takes off!

Where are these travelers going?
Match the people waiting in the ticket
line with their destination. Use the objects that the
people are carrying and their clothing as clues.

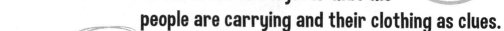
Travel Time

1 ___

TICKETS

8 ___

4 ___

3 ___

5 ___

2 ___

6 ___

7 ___

9 ___

DESTINATIONS

A

B

C

D

E

F

G

H

I

Picture Park

Can you find the words hidden in the tree? Look across, up, down, backwards, and diagonally. All the words listed below are pictured on this page.

```
              R I B F
          A I C E C R E A M
        W D T R T E O E N D
      I O A E T T S I O P C L
      G A A N T R O T D A L B H
      B A S K E T B A L L E D N
    N F L O W E R S R A O U R S
    S I T H R S E M N E C R W I K
    S L A N U I T K E K T I S K
    Q I T N P E L F L N A I C
    E U D N T E L I G O T I A
      I E U T N S N E N A D
      E R U O E H P O N D
        S R T F I N
      E E L N G
    P C Y G P
    I I C L O
    C N C Y L
    N I B E
    C C B X
```

dog   runners   fountain   picnic
ice cream   squirrel   kite   teeter-totter
bench   bicycle   pond   radio
trees   fishing pole   watermelon   swing set
blanket   basketball   flowers   cooler
                                    slide   duck

The bugs at your picnic have a message for you. Use the key to fill in the blanks.

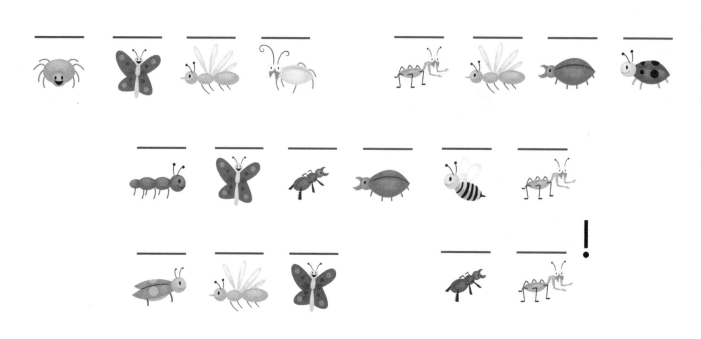

KEY

B   C   D   E   F   M   O   P   R   S   U

Mom brought home a souvenir from her trip to New York City. Connect the dots in order from 1 to 71 to find out what it is.

.34
35. .33
36. .32
.31 .30
30. .37
34. 10 28 .29 16 .14 .12
41. 27 .26 18
42. .25
43 25
.24 19. 17 15 13 .10 .9
11 .8
44. .7
23. 22
45. 21 20 .6
5. 3
46. .47 .4 .2
48. 71 .1
49. .70
.50 67 .69
66 .68
.51
.65
52.
.64
.53 .63
55. .54 .57 .62
56 58 59 60 .61

· I ♥ NY ·

Headline Adventure

Create your own wacky news story. Ask somebody for words
to fill in the blanks below. Then read the story aloud.

It was a _____ night and the _____ family was driving down the
           ADJECTIVE   NAME

highway on their way to _____. All of a sudden, they saw _____
                              PLACE   NUMBER

_____ along the side of the highway. They decided to _____
   PLURAL NOUN   VERB

because it seemed like the right thing to do. _____ decided to call for a
                                                     NAME

little _____ and everyone else started _____. When the _____
         NOUN   -ING WORD   NOUN

arrived, everything was under control. A passerby said, "It certainly was lucky that

this _____ family was driving by. Those kids knew exactly what to do in a
        ADJECTIVE

_____ like this. The kids admitted, "We were _____, and it was a
     NOUN   ADJECTIVE

great adventure, but now to have to get _____.
                                             -ING WORD

Picture Postcard

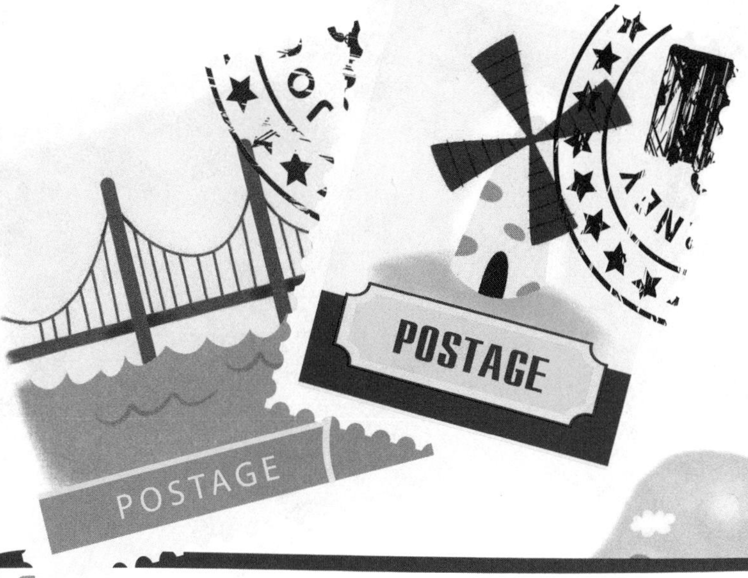
POSTAGE
POSTAGE

On one side of the postcard, draw a picture from your trip. On the other side, write all about it.

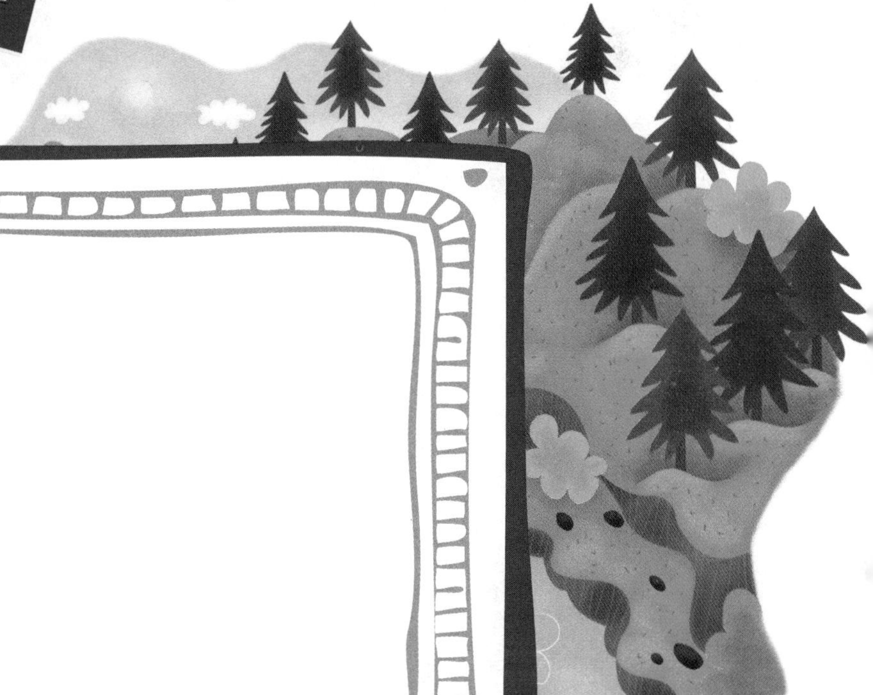

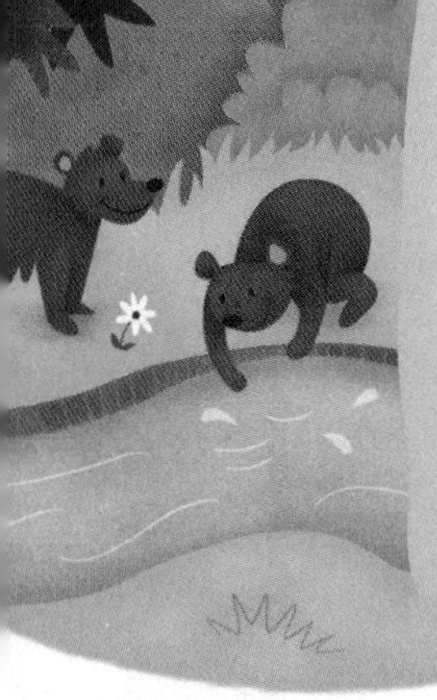

POSTAGE

To: ____________________

____

____

____

Travel Journal

Today is _____

I am in _____

Best thing I did today: _____

Worst thing I did today: _____

_____

Other Stuff

FUN-O-METER
TODAY IS...

FUN

NOT

- WORDS FAIL!
- TOTALLY AWESOME
- COOL
- PRETTY FUN
- OK
- ZERO FUN
- BIG PAIN

MOOD CHECK
Today I feel...

- ☐ Cheerful
- ☐ Helpful
- ☐ Homesick
- ☐ Dopey
- ☐ Grumpy
- ☐ Sleepy
- ☐ Bashful
- ☐ Silly
- ☐ Bored
- ☐ Other

Weather -OR- NOT

Today's weather is...

Travel Tips

What are your favorite travel tips?
DRAW your own favorites
or use ours!

Stake out your territory.

Show off your map
reading skills.

Stay energized!

Summer Vacation Crossword Puzzle

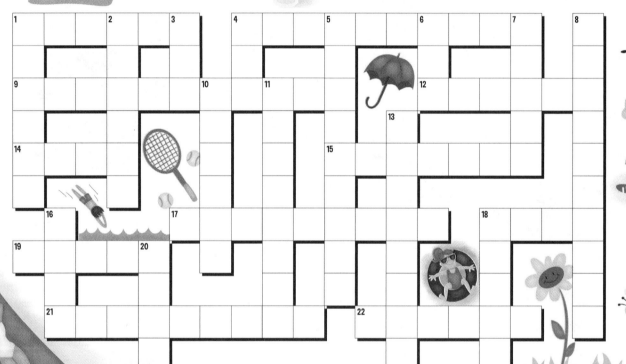

ACROSS

1. Pool of rain in the street
4. Wheeled plank that "surfs" on sidewalk
9. Car without a roof
12. Short-sleeved cotton garment
14. Grassy area around a house
15. Napping spot that swings between two trees
17. Person who polices the beach
18. Inner _____ (fun float toy)
19. Crashing breakers at the ocean
21. Grass-watering sprayer
22. Rose or daisy

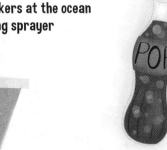

DOWN

1. Spiced cucumber sometimes eaten on hamburgers
2. Plunging into a pool off the board
3. Serving of corn on the cob
4. Water _____ ("ride" behind a boat)
5. Play home in the branches
6. Umpire's word in baseball
7. What to do when you're thirsty
8. Large, seedy summer fruit
10. Sport played with rackets and a net
11. To grill meat
13. Provides shade at the beach
16. Results of sitting in the sun
18. What to sit on at the beach
20. To jump rope

Tip-Top Travel Shop

Can you find 30 things in this scene that start with the letter T? Finding 15 is tricky, 20 is terrific, and 25 or more is tip-top.

SMILE

TAMPA

TORONTO

TUESDAY
2 MAY

$10

Make me a map

The mapmaker went home early without finishing her job!
She drew 15 states, but forgot to label them.
Can you match the states with their names?

1. Florida   _____

2. Michigan   _____

3. Oklahoma   _____

4. Ohio   _____

5. Louisiana   _____

6. California   _____

7. Hawaii   _____

8. Nevada   _____

9. Virginia   _____

10. Tennessee   _____

11. Washington   _____

12. New York   _____

13. Utah   _____

14. Massachusetts _____

15. Idaho   _____

A B C

D E F

G H I

J K L

M N O

Auto Repair

This car needs a tune up. Can you unscramble the 14 parts listed below?

1. STRINGEE LEWEH _____
2. HODO _____
3. LACEORCRATE _____
4. KNURT _____
5. SWINDLEHID _____
6. BAKER _____
7. BRASHADDO _____

8. HEWEL _____
9. RIGHTSAFE _____
10. GENNIE _____
11. LADHEIGHT _____
12. BURPEM _____
13. ELFMURF _____
14. TYRETAB _____

Something's Fishy

Can you spot at least 10 differences between the top and bottom fish tanks?

Surf's Up!

Can you find 10 things wrong with this picture?

Travel Log

Write your own "been there, done that" lists under the headings below.

I've been THERE

I've DONE that

I'd like to go there

I NEVER want to go there

Wacky water park

Call the lifeguard! There's a whale in the swimming pool. That's not the only thing wrong at this water park. Look at the picture to find 11 other strange things.

89

On the Right Track

BOXCAR

BRAKEMAN

CABOOSE

CARGO

CATTLECAR

CHOO-CHOO

CONDUCTOR

CROSSING

ENGINEER

EXPRESS

LOCOMOTIVE

MONORAIL

PULLMAN

RAILROAD

ROUNDHOUSE

SIGNAL

TIES

TUNNEL

WHISTLE

```
                    T R N       L R A                   S T P
                    O A C       O C A                   I O O
              L E M O L R C E A   I B Y A S   G V L
              S E I T H T O S N R L R L O A   N E L   B
              S K A N I N C M S S G G R N O N E L M   O
          I S A R O U N D H O U S E I O O B   A N X C
          O R S C O N D U C T O R I R N E A   B T E A L
          B W H I S T L E T I I H A N P E C   E A A L
          R A C E L T T A C V F I C E G X E   C D R R
              G A T         H E L           A   E E E V
              C H R         I S T           I     R
                                                  A   A V
                                                  E   I E
```

The 19 words listed to the left are hidden in the train. Look across, back, up, down, and diagonally to find them.

Bloomers

How many flowers can you name using the word pictures below?

1.  [butter dish] + [cup] =

2.  [pans] + E =

3.  [snap] + [dragon] =

4.  [car] + [nation] =

5.  [fox] + [glove] =

6.  APRIL + e =

7.   [cows] + [lips] =

8.  [24K gold] + n + [fishing rod] =

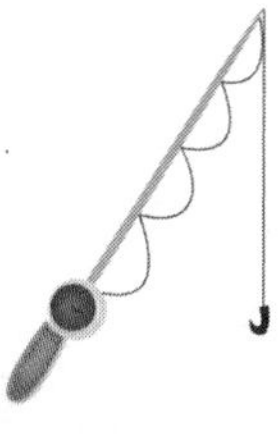

Pathways

Juan wants to go fishing, Michelle wants to do some bird watching, and Keisha wants to go rock climbing. Which trail should each person take?

92

Winter Vacation

Crossword Puzzle

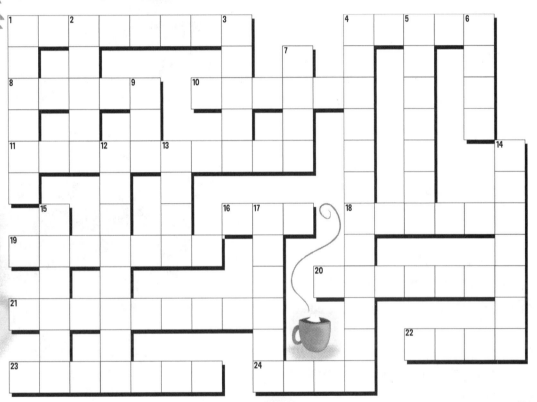

ACROSS

1. Hanukkah and Thanksgiving are two
4. Sled-pulling dog
8. Apple drink
10. Light coat
11. Pine trees, for instance
16. Head covering
18. Wax with a wick
19. Warm fabric for sheets or pajamas
20. Bed covering
21. Where to burn logs indoors
22. Twinkling light in the sky
23. Container that keeps drinks hot
24. The North _____ (Santa's home)

DOWN

1. Game played with a puck
2. Cozy inn
3. To glide on ice with blades
4. Sweet, warm drink
5. Frosty, for instance
6. Holiday word with log or -tide
7. Downhill or cross-country gliders
9. Floor covering
12. Rudolph, for instance
13. Travel on a snowmobile
14. Warm, knitted pullover
15. Sledded carrier pulled by horses
17. Hibernating

Highway Robbery

It was late in the afternoon as we sped along the dusty road in the family station wagon. We were on our way to Florida for our annual family vacation and my little sister Louise was really starting to get on my nerves. We were nearly to Chattanooga when the station wagon slowed down.

"What's going on?" my mother asked.

Through the windshield I could see some sort of roadblock. We slowly crept along until we reached several police officers standing by orange cones that blocked the road. An old blue convertible had been directed over to the side of the road and one of the officers was talking with the man who owned it.

My dad rolled down his window as another police officer approached our car.

"There's been a robbery at the local grocery store ten miles away," the officer explained. "We're checking cars, because we think the robber is trying to get out of town."

We all got out of the car. I sat on the bumper, listening to the conversation between the other policeman and the man in the blue convertible. I noticed that his backseat was filled with grocery bags.

"Officer, I tell you, these are my things I bought a day ago in Salt Lake City," the man said. "I've been driving for 12 hours straight. I haven't even heard of the grocery store you're talking about."

The policeman looked skeptical. He strolled to the front of the car, took out a notepad, and began writing down the license plate number on the convertible.

The man was not telling the truth.
Do you know what gave him away?

Happy Camper?

Help make this hungry camper a happy camper. Find the hidden fork, plate, cup, cooler, sandwich, apple, bottle, and slice of cake.

Under the Big Top

Connect the dots in order from 1 to 109 to find out what the girl is riding.

Message in the Sand

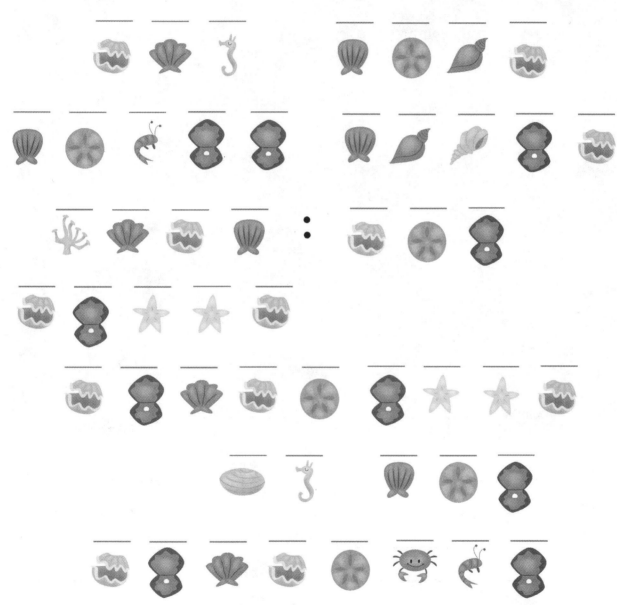

KEY

A B E F H I L M O R S T Y

Barnyard SCRAMBLE

How many of the 14 animal names can you unscramble?
All of the animals are pictured on this page.

1. GDO _____

2. ACT _____

3. OWC _____

4. ADOT _____

5. KUCD _____

6. TOGA _____

7. ORCW _____

8. OGSOE _____

9. EOMUS _____

10. SHOER _____

11. NOBRI _____

12. BRITAB _____

13. NARCOCO _____

14. RLIQEUSR _____

Backseat BINGO!

This game can be played with up to four people. Select a bingo card. Each time you see one of the items pictured on the card, draw an X on that square. The first person to cross out five squares across, down or diagonally wins.

Your friends have run off to their favorite rides at the amusement park.
Use the nine squares below as hints to help you find your friends.

BUMPER CARS

TONS-O-FUN
AMUSEMENT PARK

100

Travel Journal

I am in _____

Today is _____

Best thing I did today: _____

Worst thing I did today: _____

_____

_____

Other Stuff

FUN-O-METER
TODAY IS...

FUN ↑

NOT ↓

- WORDS FAIL!
- TOTALLY AWESOME
- COOL
- PRETTY FUN
- OK
- ZERO FUN
- BIG PAIN

MOOD CHECK
Today I feel...

☐ Cheerful
☐ Helpful
☐ Homesick
☐ Dopey
☐ Grumpy
☐ Sleepy
☐ Bashful
☐ Silly
☐ Bored
☐ Other

Weather -OR- NOT

Today's weather is...

101

Fantasy Vacation

What's the best vacation you can imagine? Maybe it's sailing on the ocean, racing down the slopes, or even blasting off into space. Draw a picture of your very own fantasy vacation below.

Movie Set Match-up

There has been a mix-up on the movie set. See if you can help by matching the actors with their vehicles. Use the objects that the actors are carrying and their clothes as clues.

2. ___

3. ___

4. ___

5. ___

6. ___

7. ___

8. ___

9. ___

10. ___

PROPS

MAIL

A

B

C

D

E

F

G

H

I

J

FINISH

Start pedaling in Cape Cod, Massachusetts, and coast across the finish line in California. Watch out! There may be a few dead ends in your path.

The race is ON!

START

105

Plane Challenge

See if you can find a place in the puzzle for all of the words listed below. The numbers show you how many letters are in each word. Here's a hint: Start with the words that have 12, 14, or 16 letters in them. (Spaces between words don't count!)

3
hub
nap
sky

4
gate
ramp
soda
tags

5
aisle
coach
hotel
novel
pilot
seats
snack

6
laptop
pillow
on time
snooze
ticket

7
airport
blanket
co-pilot
deplane
parking
peanuts

8
airspeed
landings
navigate
schedule
takeoffs

9
concourse
passenger

10
first class
flight plan
turbulence

11
folding tray
landing gear

12
baggage check

13
inflight movie
ticket counter

14
carry-on luggage

15
baggage carousel
crossword puzzle
flight attendant

16
cruising altitude

Bicycle Mix-up

Looks like a bicycle mix-up. Can you find 10 other things wrong with this picture?

BUY & BUY

You have exactly 205 tickets to spend on prizes. If you want to spend exactly all of your tickets and you don't want to buy more than one of anything, which items should you buy?

PRIZES

NECKLACES 80 TICKETS

POLISHED ROCKS 35 TICKETS

POSTCARDS 25 TICKETS

KEY RINGS 95 TICKETS

WINDUP TOY 50 TICKETS

GIANT PENCIL 70 TICKETS

CANDY 15 TICKETS

GLASSES 200 TICKETS

Which HOTEL?

It's getting late and the Tyred family needs to find their hotel. They know it's on Yawn Avenue, but which hotel is it? Mr. Tyred stayed here years ago and remembers the facts below. Use them to figure out where the family should check in before everyone falls asleep.

 **FACTS:**

1. The hotel has a circular driveway.
2. The number on the hotel is even.
3. The hotel is between two hotels that have palm trees in front of them.
4. The name of the hotel (without the word "inn" or "hotel") spells another word when it is written backwards.

ZANY ZOO

Can you spot 10 differences between the top and bottom scenes?

While-you-wait BINGO!

BINGO!

This game can be played with up to four people. Select a bingo card. Each time you see one of the items pictured on the card, draw an X on that square. The first person to cross out five squares across, down or diagonally wins.

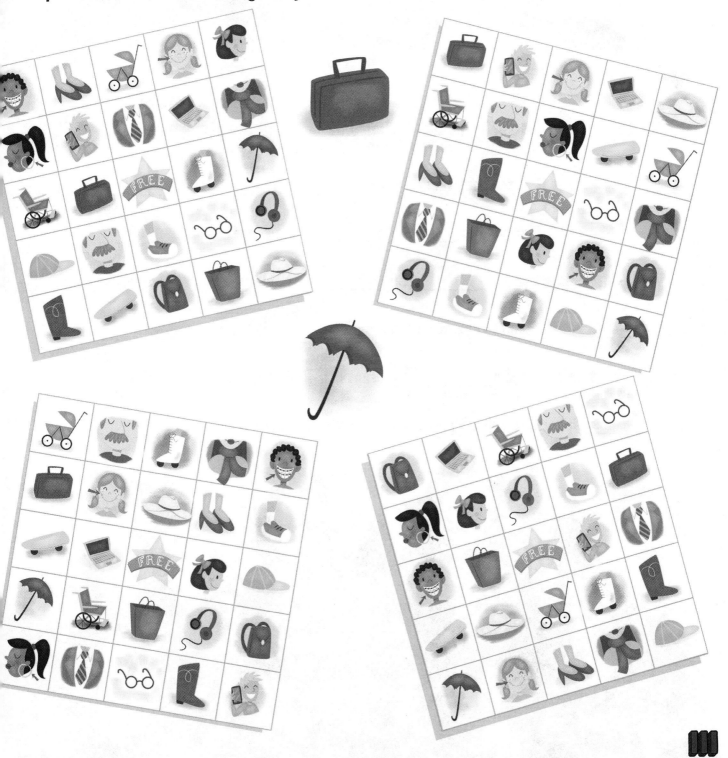

Best Vacation EVER!

Create your own crazy story. Ask somebody for words to fill in the blanks below. Then read the story aloud.

_____ says that the best vacation ever is a _____ trip to _____.
PERSON'S NAME   NOUN   PLACE

Once you're there, you just have to _____. And don't forget to _____. The most
VERB   VERB

exciting things to do are _____ and _____, but only if you're wearing _____.
ACTIVITY   ACTIVITY   TYPE OF CLOTHING

There's _____ food to eat, too. Order the _____ and _____ special
ADJECTIVE   NOUN   NOUN

for a real treat, and tell them _____ sent you. Before you head home, be sure to buy a
PERSON'S NAME

_____ at the souvenir shop! It will always remind you of your _____ trip.
NOUN   ADJECTIVE

Travel Journal

I am in _____

Today is _____

Best thing I did today: _____

Worst thing I did today: _____

_____

_____

Other Stuff

MOOD CHECK

Today I feel...

☐ Cheerful
☐ Helpful
☐ Homesick
☐ Dopey
☐ Grumpy
☐ Sleepy
☐ Bashful
☐ Silly
☐ Bored
☐ Other

Weather -OR- NOT

Today's weather is...

☐ ☐
☐ ☐

Thumbs UP/Thumbs DOWN

List the best
of your trip
on this side.

List the worst
on this side.

Things
to do

Souvenirs

People
I've
met

Food &
Restaurants

Places
to go

Soup's On

How many foods can you name using the pictures below?
You'll have to add and subtract letters or words to find the answers.

1. 🫛 + 🌰 + 🧈 + & + 🍄 – 🐟 =

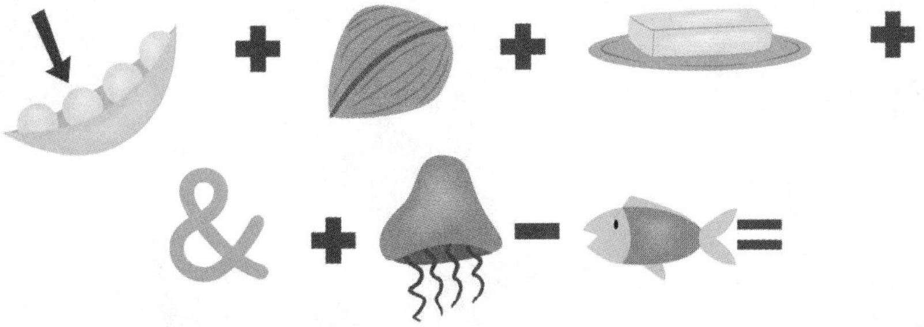

2. BLAH BLAH BLAH + O =

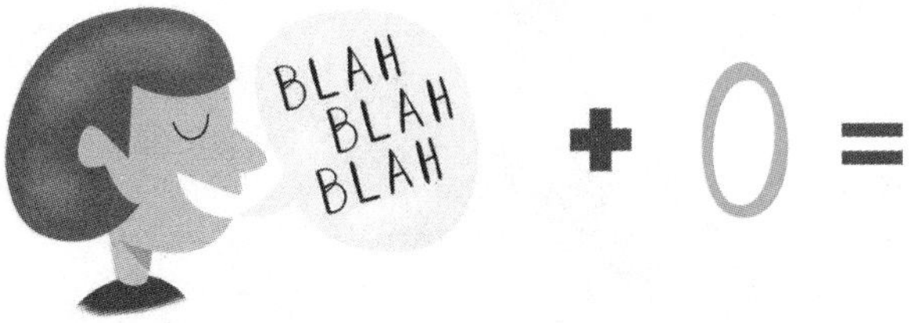

3. M + 🗑 – B + A + 🛶 + 🦵 + & + 🧀 =

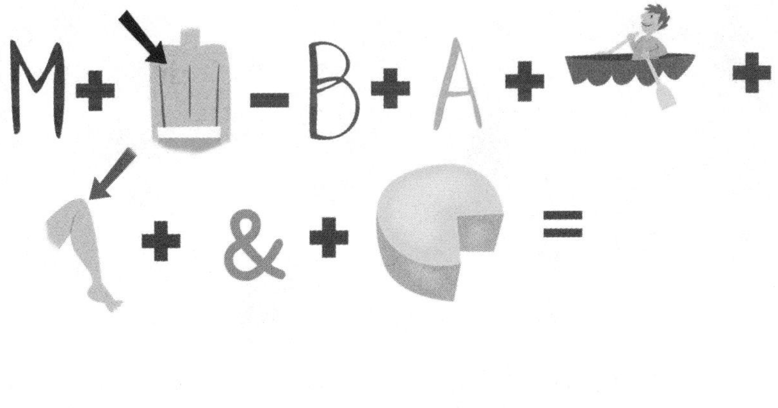

4. 🐶 – T + G + 🧺 – N + I =

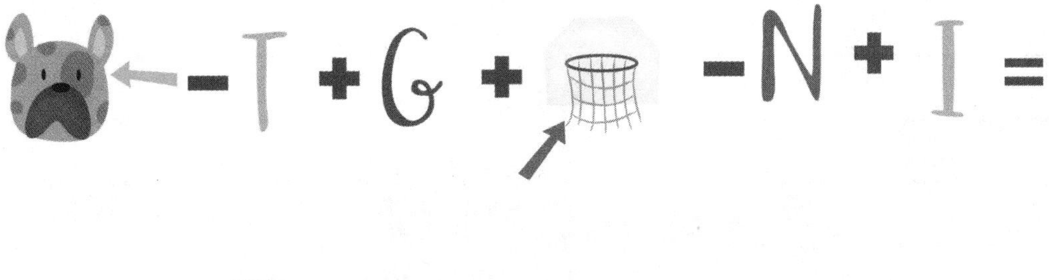

5. 🌰 + ⛰ – 🧊 + 🧸 – F =

115

Stormy Seas

How many of these words can you unscramble? All 13 sea-going vessels are pictured above.

1. KAR _____

2. PISH _____

3. FRAT _____

4. OCEAN _____

5. CHATY _____

6. YAKKA _____

7. REBAG _____

8. BUGATTO _____

9. LOANDOG _____

10. ALSOBAIT _____

11. BRAINMUSE _____

12. WEIRDSNURF _____

13. CARRIFAT RICERRA _____

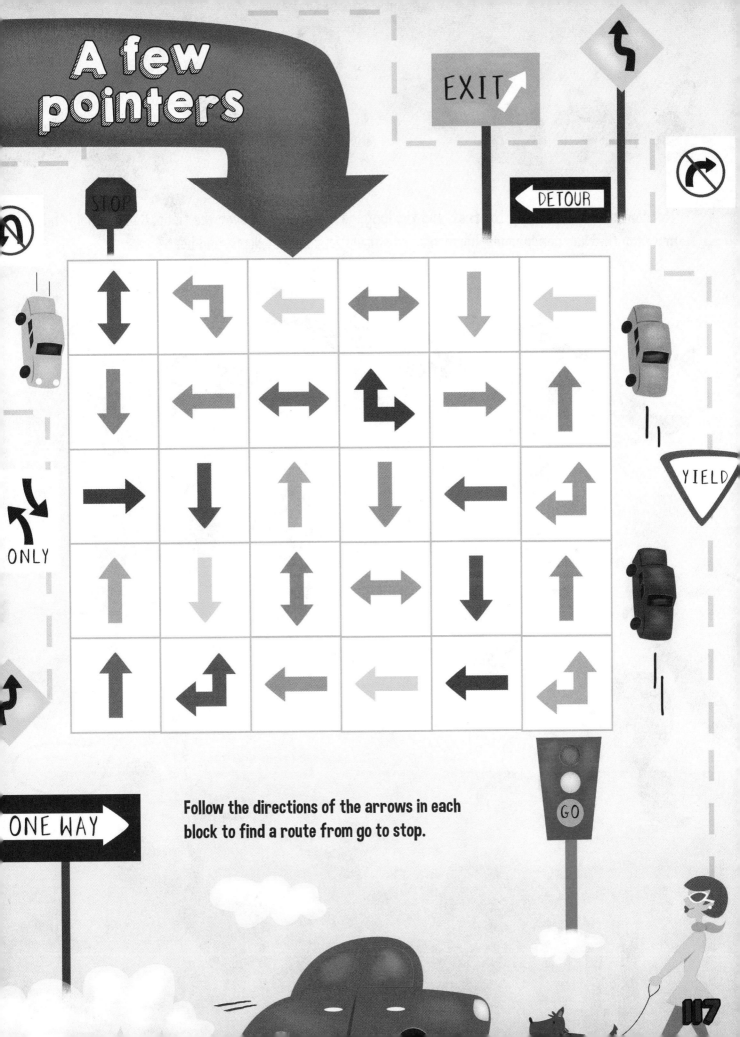

A few pointers

Follow the directions of the arrows in each block to find a route from go to stop.

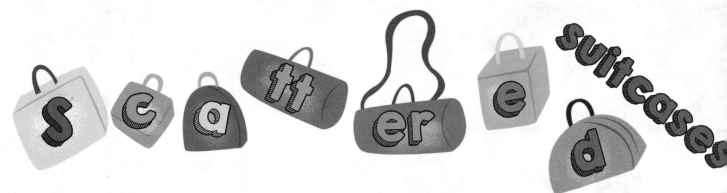

scattered suitcases

The conveyor belt is going too fast, and the luggage has spilled all over the floor. Can you help the musician find her headphones, harmonica, sheet music, compact discs, and horn?

Mini-mystery

SEA BREEZE HOTEL

Pooltime Puzzler

It was a sunny morning and I was lounging by the pool at our hotel. We had arrived in Florida yesterday and were taking it easy. The drive to Florida had taken longer than usual, because we got stuck in a roadblock on the way down.

My dad was in the pool, splashing around with my little sister Louise. My mom was stretched out on the lounge chair next to me, reading a book.

"Plunk." A tall woman with flaming red hair and long, sparkly earrings sat down in the chair on the other side of me.

"How ya doin,' darlin'?" she asked in a slow drawl. "I'm visiting my son, who moved here last year from our home state of North Carolina."

"I'm here with my mom and dad...and my little sister," I said.

"Oh, a sister," the lady said, "that's nice. Girls run in my family, too. I don't have a brother, but I do have a sister, who has no children." She continued, "My sister's father had a wife whose mother had a great grandaughter with a twin sister. But, the twins had no brothers."

Across the pool, someone yelled to the lady. "Peaches, I'm ready to go."

The lady smiled, got up, and said, "It's a nickname my son has for me. You know, like the nickname of my home state. Now you have a nice visit down here and take care of your little sister."

She walked away and I turned to my mom: "The lady with the red hair has a lot of imagination. But she doesn't have a son and she isn't from North Carolina."

Do you know how I figured this out?

dot-to-dot...
Down Under

Connect the dots in order from 1 to 87 to find out what's pulling the carriage.

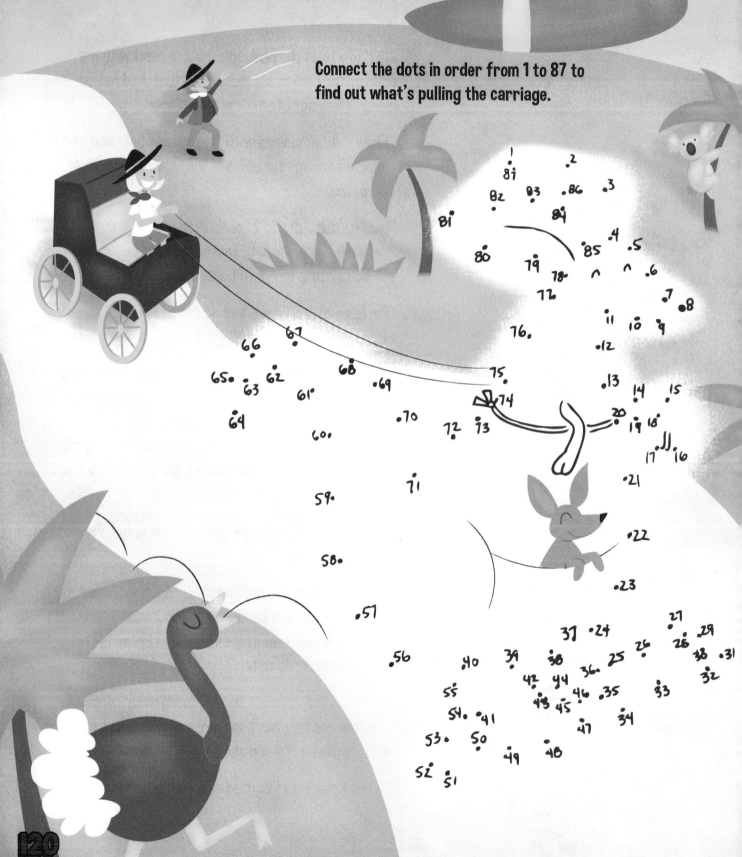

Skiing Double

A.

B.

C.

D.

E.

F.

G.

H.

Can you spot the two skiers that are exactly alike?

Up, up & away!

```
                          U
              P  J  E  T     W
              E  L  S  I  A
              S  G  T  O  I
              O  N  I  M  G
              O  E  M  G  N
              T  H  A  T  I
              E  B  T  T
R A D A R T E K C I T E E W W E A T H E R W E R C
I A I R P O R T C L O U D S S C H E D U L E L D B
P I L L O W F F O E K A T U R B U L E N C E W O R
T I P K C O C E N I L R I A L U B T H G I L F E Y
O E M I T L A N D I N G M I P L A V I R R A H O P
                    N  D  E  R  E
                    K  E  O  P  A
                    R  C  F  L  N
                    F  L  A  A  U
                    R  Y  R  N  T
                    E  I  R  E  S
    Y  K  S  G  N  I  Y  L  F  N  G
    H  I  G  N  A  V  I  G  A  T  E
    H  I  D  E  P  A  R  T  U  R  E
    N  T  O  S  S  L  N  I  B  A  C
    S  T  G  H  E
    A  S  K  A  Y
    P  I  L  O  T
```

flying
gate
hop
hub

clouds
cockpit
crew
departure
estimated time of arrival
flight

jet
landing
navigate
passenger

seat
sky
snack
tags
takeoff
ticket

aisle
airline
airplane
airport
arrival
bags
cabin

peanuts
pillow
pilot
radar
row
schedule

time
turbulence
weather
wings

All of the words listed in the clouds are hidden in the airplane. Look
across, down, up, backwards, and diagonally to find them.

122

Where's my mummy?

You're lost in the museum. Can you find your way from the dinosaurs to the gift shop?

ENTER HERE

GIFT SHOP

Hide and Seek

These kids are playing hide and seek in their hotel room. Can you spy these items hidden in the room with them: a magnifying glass, umbrella, snake, hot dog, skateboard, baseball cap, book, and donut?

Flag Code

Use the International Flag Code to solve the riddle below.

A B C D E F G H I J K L M

N O P Q R S T U V W X Y Z

?

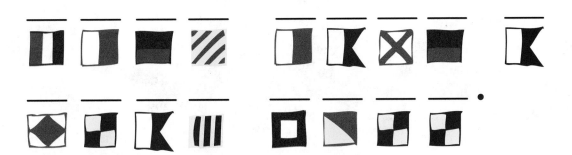

.

I SPY

If you are "it," choose an object, like a red button, and say, "I spy with my little eye something red." The other players then take turns trying to guess what the object is. The person who guesses the answer gets to be "it." HINT: Don't give the answer away by staring at the object.

NAME THAT TUNE

Players take turns thinking of songs and humming them for one another, a few notes at a time, while the others try to be the first to "name that tune." Once you have a tune in mind, hum just the first three notes. If nobody recognizes it, hum the first four notes. Keep adding notes, one at a time, until someone guesses the name of the song. The first person to guess becomes the next "hummer." (Good whistlers can whistle their tunes.)

MAKE ME LAUGH

This game is serious fun. No kidding! One person becomes the "jester" and the rest are "stonefaces." Stonefaces must never laugh or smile—if they do, their faces break. Of course the jester thinks this is funny and likes nothing more than to make stonefaces crack up. That's the game! The jester has to crack up the stonefaces. The jester can make faces, funny noises, tell jokes, but cannot tickle or touch the stonefaces to make them laugh. The last stoneface to laugh gets to be the next jester.

ROCHAMBEAU

This game, sometimes called "Rock, Paper, Scissors," works best with two or three players. These are the rules—paper (flat hand) covers rock, rock (fist) breaks scissors, and scissors (move first two fingers like scissors) cut paper. All players put their fists out together to the beat of Rochambeau (Ro—Sham—Bo). On "Bo," each player forms either rock, paper, or scissors. Then everybody has to follow the rules.

CITY TRAIN

If you know the names of a lot of cities, take a ride on the City Train. The rules are simple—players take turns saying the names of cities. The only catch is that each city name must begin with the letter that ended the last one. For example, Houston might be followed by New York, which might be followed by Kansas City, and so on. Any player who can't come up with a city has to get off the train. The last one riding the City Train is the winner. All aboard!

Travel Games

A—MY NAME IS...

Here's a "fill in the blank" game that works its way through the alphabet. It's best when the pressure of keeping the rhythm going makes players work especially hard. Here's how a boy might start things off beginning with the letter A: A—my name is Abner, my sister's name is Anne, we come from Alaska and we sell Axes." A girl might follow, "B—my name is Bertha, my brother's name is Bert, we come from Boston and we sell beans." You get the idea—you're out when you can't complete the sentence or when you break the tempo.

1

2

3

PLATE-O-GRAMS

This game has no winner or losers—just some funny messages. To start, somebody has to spot a license plate and read the letters on the plate to everyone. For example, the letters might be "B—R—G." Next, everyone thinks of a three-word message beginning with those letters. In this case, people might come up with "<u>B</u>ig <u>R</u>ound <u>G</u>lobs" or "<u>B</u>eware <u>R</u>abid <u>G</u>erbils." (You might want to allow "little" words so the plate-o-grams make more sense, for example, "My <u>B</u>rother is <u>R</u>eally <u>G</u>ross.")

A

B

ALPHABET DERBY

This is a race to the end of the alphabet. To play, you must find all the letters of the alphabet—in order. Letters may be found on road signs, billboards, bumper stickers, license plates, etc. You don't have to announce each letter you find, but if asked, you must tell what letter you are on. If challenged, you should be able to say where you saw your letters. The first one to Z wins. (To make things go more quickly, you may want to agree that Q is the only letter that can be found out of order.)

C

BUZZ

If you've got a head for numbers, buzz is for you. First, players pick a number from 2 through 9. That number becomes buzz. Once buzz is named, players take turns counting, starting with 1. If buzz is 3, whenever you get to a number that contains a 3 or is a multiple of 3, you must say buzz. Players who mess up are out and counting starts over again from 1. The last player remaining wins. For a challenge, play bizz-buzz, picking two numbers instead of just one. One number is bizz, and the other is buzz.

CATEGORIES

This game is good for many ages, since it can be made as easy or as difficult as you want. It all has to do with categories. One person thinks of a category—any category. It could be colors, capital cities, sports teams, or anything you can think of. Then players take turns naming items in the category. The game ends when someone repeats something already mentioned, or when players can't think of any other items in the category.

20 QUESTIONS

This old standby is simple, but fun. One player thinks of something (anything you can see, smell, hear, or touch) and tells the others if it is an animal, vegetable, or mineral. The others take turns asking "yes-or-no" questions to try to figure out what it is. At any time a player may use a turn to guess what it is. It's best to ask a lot of questions before you start guessing, but remember, you only have twenty questions. Whoever guesses right wins. You can play this game using other categories, too, like famous people, places, etc. Be creative!

Songs to drive

The Twelve Days of Our Trip
(to the tune of "The Twelve Days of Christmas")

On the first day of our trip this is what I saw—the baby threw up in the car.

On the second day of our trip this is what I saw—two pick-up trucks and the baby threw up in the car.

Third day:
Fourth day:
Fifth day:
Sixth day:
Seventh day:
Eighth day:
Ninth day:
Tenth day:
Eleventh day:
Twelfth day:

three dead skunks
four minivans
five backseat fights
six broken headlights
seven miles of road work
eight cars a-speeding
nine railroad crossings
ten roadside rest stops
eleven cop cars hiding
twelve bumper stickers

99 Miles to Go on Our Trip
(to the tune of "99 Bottles")

99 miles to go on our trip.
99 miles to go.
Step on the gas. I think we can pass.
98 miles to go on our trip...

(Keep repeating until you get to "0 miles to go" or until someone kicks you out of the car, whichever comes first.)

Backseat Border Blues
(to the tune of "This Land is Your Land")

This side is my side; that side is your side.
Let's get along now; this is a long ride.
You see this line here—please don't cross over.
One side for you and one for me.

I had my eyes closed—faked I was sleeping.
So you got greedy and started creeping.
Try that again, Bub, and you'll be weeping.
One side for you and one for me.

Just like I warned you—now you are crying.
And Dad is angry—now you are lying.
You had it coming, there's no denying.
One side for you and one for me.

grown-ups CRAZY!

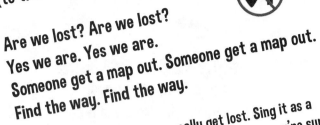

Are We Lost?
(to the tune of "Are you Sleeping?")

Are we lost? Are we lost?
Yes we are. Yes we are.
Someone get a map out. Someone get a map out.
Find the way. Find the way.

(Save this one for when you really get lost. Sing it as a round—as you drive around and around—and you're sure to drive the grown-ups crazy.)

Don't Get Out of the Fast Lane
(to the tune of "Take Me Out to the Ball Game")

Don't get out of the fast lane.
Don't let up on the gas.
I can't believe all the cars we've passed—
Wherever we're going, we're going there fast.
And it's zoom, zoom, zoom down the freeway.
But don't break the speed limit please.
Or the friend-ly Highway Patrol
Will request your keys!

Battle Hymn of the Brat
(to the tune of "Battle Hymn of the Republic")

Our minivan is loaded to the roof with games and toys.
We've all had snacks and found a station everyone enjoys.
The kids are all behaving well; we've hardly made a noise.
But something's not quite right.

(Chorus)
I'M NOT HAVING ANY FUN YET.
I'M NOT HAVING ANY FUN YET.
I'M NOT HAVING ANY FUN YET.
THIS TRIP IS DRAGGING ON.

We've hit every tourist trap from Maine to Monterey.
Miami to Mount Rushmore, Plymouth Rock to Frisco Bay.
We wait in never-ending lines forever and a day.
It's time to take a rest.

(Chorus)

Now you might think that I'm spoiled, that my attitude is bad.
You wouldn't be the first if my complaining makes you mad
In fact you'd be the third, behind my Mother and my Dad.
But I still feel like this:

(Chorus)

When-You-Get-There

Paper Airplane Games

Find some paper and follow the paper airplane instructions. Then you can play games with your paper planes. 1) Go for distance. Whose plane can fly the farthest? 2) Fly for accuracy. Who can land closest to a chosen target? 3) Stay aloft. Whose plane can stay in the air the longest?

①
FOLD, THEN
UNFOLD ON
①

②
FOLD DOWN CORNERS
FOLD DOWN ON LINE **②**

FOLD DOWN
CORNERS AGAI

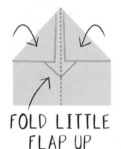

FOLD LITTLE
FLAP UP

FOLD THIS SIDE
BACK TO MEET
OTHER SIDE

FOLD WINGS DOWN
ON BOTH SIDES

Hide the Doohickey

Any small object will do in this game. It's fun for kids of all ages. One player hides the object while the others wait in another room. Players are then called back to find the object. Younger players might need to be told if they are "warm" or "cold." The first player to find the object gets to hide it next.

Bright Ideas

If you have a flashlight, you will never be bored again, at least not until you wear the battery out. Set up a flashlight in a dark room and make hand shadow figures on the wall. Tell a scary story while projecting a spider or a ghost onto the ceiling. Cut out shadow puppets and put on a show. With more than one flashlight you can play flashlight tag after dark—instead of tagging people, you hit them with your beam of light. A flashlight can also add a scary touch to face-making. Turn out the lights and see how scary you can look!

Learn to Girn

Face facts, faces are funny. Take your face to a mirror and see just how funny it can get. Serious face-makers call it "girning." It's even funnier if you have someone else to girn with. Work on blinks, winks, sneers, grimaces, grins, eyebrow raises, sidelong glances, etc. How many emotions can you show? How many faces can you make?

GAMES

Wastebasket H-O-R-S-E

A wastebasket makes a good indoor basketball hoop, and horse is a good indoor game. In horse, players take turns shooting for the hoop from various places on the court. Use rolled-up socks, crumpled-up paper or an appropriate indoor ball. If a player makes a shot the next player must make it too. One miss, and you get an H, two misses, an H-O; and so on. Miss five times and you are out with H-O-R-S-E.

Sock Soccer

This game is just like it sounds. Roll up some socks, set up some goals, agree on a rule or two, and start kicking. (WARNING: According to the American Sock Soccer Association, using lamps and plants for goalposts can get you in an awful lot of trouble!)

Slo-mo Volleyball

If you have any balloons left over from the water balloon toss, fill one with air for this slow motion indoor version of volleyball. Play on your knees using a bed, couch, or some chairs for a net. You give up a point when you hit the balloon out, let it touch the ground, or fail to get it over in the agreed upon number of hits. Spike it, dude, but don't let it pop!

Water Balloon Toss

In this damp contest, players pair up and form two lines facing each other. Each pair gets a balloon. One at a time, one person in each pair tosses the balloon to the other. After each successful toss, the tosser backs up a full step. The pair completing the longest toss wins and gets to stay dry! Most grown-ups will insist that you play this game outside.

Whirly-Bird

Make a simple paper helicopter using the instructions. Decorate your whirly-bird with markers or crayons before you cut it out. Drop your whirly-bird from a high place. When the wind is right, your whirly-bird will stay in the air for a long time. Watch it land, and then be sure to get it and fly it again.

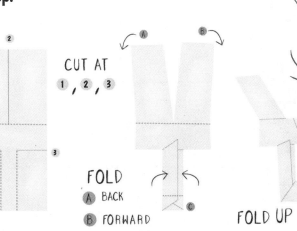

CUT AT
1, 2, 3

FOLD
A BACK
B FORWARD
C AS SHOWN

FOLD UP

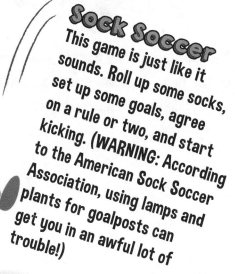

Where oh where?

The pictures below appear somewhere in this book—but where? Find each picture and write the title of the page it appears on in the blanks. Then write the circled letters in order at the bottom of the page to decode the hidden message.

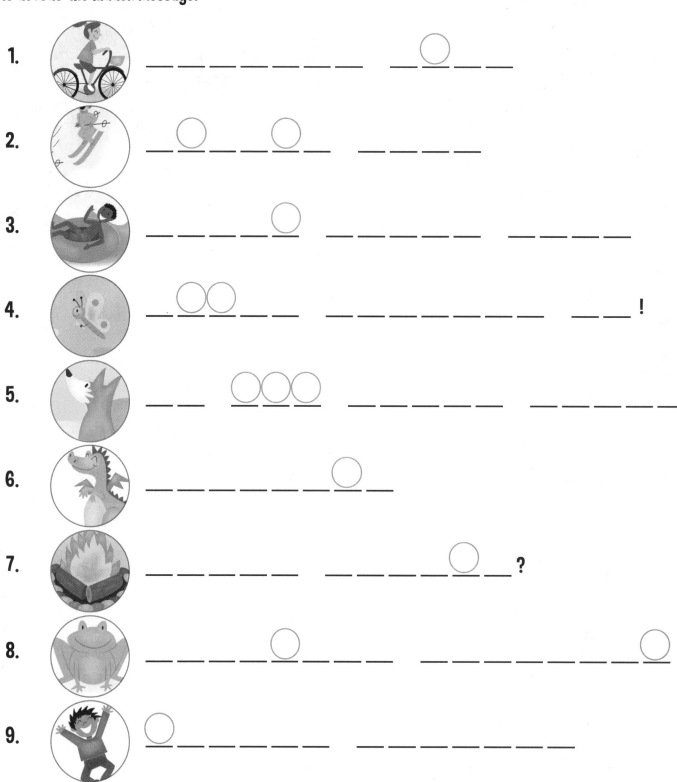

1. _ _ _ _ _ _ _ _   _ ◯ _ _

2. _ ◯ _ _ ◯ _ _   _ _ _ _

3. _ _ _ _ _ ◯ _   _ _ _ _ _   _ _ _ _

4. _ ◯◯ _ _ _   _ _ _ _ _ _   _ _!

5. _ _   ◯◯◯ _ _   _ _ _ _ _   _ _ _ _ _

6. _ _ _ _ _ ◯ _ _

7. _ _ _ _ _   _ _ _ _ ◯ _?

8. _ _ _ _ _ ◯ _ _ _   _ _ _ _ _ _ ◯

9. ◯ _ _ _ _ _ _   _ _ _ _ _ _ _

_ _ _   _ _ _   _ _ _ _ _   _ _ _?

Contents

With *Coast-to-Coast Games* you can discover exciting new adventures, coast to coast and border to border within the United States. Check out the great scenery and terrific things to see and do, and meet some interesting people. It's time to explore these fun kid-friendly places along the way.

This book will tell you about many of these places. Read a little, play the games, and pretend that you are there. The United States map at the beginning of this book will show you where these places are located. Look into the ones that are near your home, or plan to visit the places that seem fun to you. Be sure to watch for the little red bird throughout this book for special surprises.

The travel games will make the time fly as you ride along in the car or fly in an airplane. Play the games alone or with other people. The games range from easy to hard, but all of them are fun. The only supplies you need are a pencil, crayons, and coins or other markers.

So grab your book and supplies, buckle up, and you're off on a great adventure "coast to coast."

© Rand McNally
M-102198-1

WASHINGTON
Seattle
Portland

Glacier N.P.

MONTANA

NORTH DA

Bismarck

Butte

Rogue River

PACIFIC
OCEAN

OREGON

IDAHO

Boise

SOUTH DAK

Rapid City

Yellowstone N.P. /
Grand Teton N.P.

WYOMING

Black Hills

NEBRAS

Great Salt
Lake

San Francisco

Lake Tahoe

NEVADA

Salt Lake City

Dinosaur N.M.

Cheyenne

Yosemite N.P.

Denver/
Colorado Springs

UTAH

CALIFORNIA

COLORADO

Kings Canyon N.P./
Sequoia N.P.

Las Vegas

Bryce Canyon N.P./
Zion N.P.

Mesa Verde
N.P.

KANS

Hoover Dam/
Lake Mead

Grand Canyon
N.P.

Santa Fe/
Taos

Los Angeles

ARIZONA

Oklahoma

San Diego

Phoenix

Albuquerque

Amarillo

NEW MEXICO

Tucson/
Tombstone

Dallas/Ft.

El Paso

RUSSIA

ALASKA

MEXICO

TEXAS

Denali N.P.

CANADA

San Antonio

Anchorage

Honolulu

PACIFIC
OCEAN

PACIFIC
OCEAN

HAWAII

Hawaii Volcanoes N.P.

136

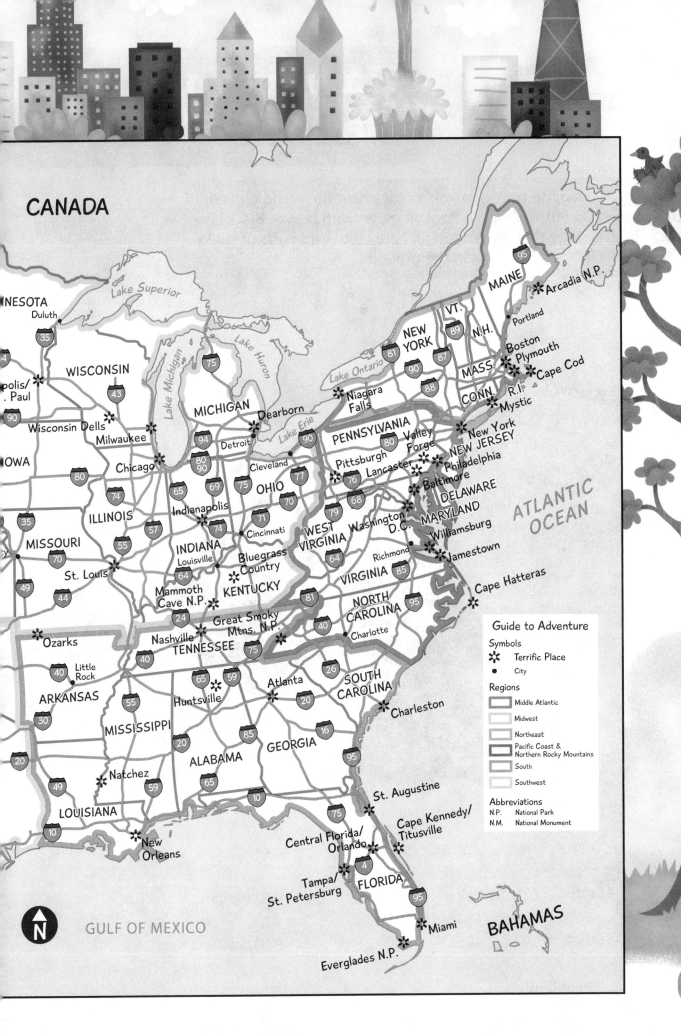

CANADA

Lake Superior

NESOTA
Duluth

35

WISCONSIN

polis/
Paul

43

90

Wisconsin Dells

Milwaukee

IOWA

80

Lake Michigan

Lake Huron

75

MICHIGAN

94

Dearborn

Detroit

Lake Erie

Cleveland

MAINE • Arcadia N.P.

95

VT.

Portland

89   N.H.

NEW
YORK

81   87

90

MASS.

Boston
Plymouth
Cape Cod

CONN.

R.I.
Mystic

88

Chicago

80
90

Niagara
Falls

PENNSYLVANIA

80

Valley
Forge

New York

65   69   75

OHIO   77

Pittsburgh

76

NEW JERSEY

74   70

Indianapolis

57

MISSOURI

35

ILLINOIS

55

70

St. Louis

49

44

Ozarks

40

Little
Rock

ARKANSAS

30

24

Louisville

64

INDIANA

Cincinnati

71

Bluegrass
Country

KENTUCKY

Mammoth
Cave N.P.

Great Smoky
Mtns. N.P.

Nashville

40

TENNESSEE

79

68

Lancaster   Philadelphia

Baltimore

DELAWARE

WEST
VIRGINIA

Washington
D.C.

MARYLAND

64

VIRGINIA

Williamsburg

Jamestown

ATLANTIC
OCEAN

Richmond

85

NORTH
CAROLINA

Cape Hatteras

81

40

95

Charlotte

75

26

Atlanta

Huntsville

65   59

20

SOUTH
CAROLINA

Charleston

55

MISSISSIPPI

20

85

GEORGIA

16

ALABAMA

49

Natchez

59

65

95

20

10

LOUISIANA

10

New
Orleans

St. Augustine

Cape Kennedy/
Titusville

Central Florida/
Orlando

75

4

Tampa/
St. Petersburg

FLORIDA

95

Guide to Adventure

Symbols

✳ Terrific Place

• City

Regions

☐ Middle Atlantic

☐ Midwest

☐ Northeast

☐ Pacific Coast &
    Northern Rocky Mountains

☐ South

☐ Southwest

Abbreviations

N.P. National Park

N.M. National Monument

N

GULF OF MEXICO

Miami

BAHAMAS

Everglades N.P.

137

Hawaii Volcanoes National Park

The volcanoes in this park give you an idea how the world looked long ago. Inside the volcano a fiery pit glows with power. Black lava rock twists its way through a strange, bare land. And puffs of stinky steam escape from the cracks in the ground.

Did You Know?

The big island of Hawaii is the youngest of the present Hawaiian islands. But, to the southeast of Hawaii, under the water, is a new volcanic island forming which should reach the surface in about 10,000 years.

Can you identify the parts of a volcano?

Cinder cone_____   Lava_____

Crater_____   Magma_____

Eruption_____   Vent_____

Gas and ash_____   Volcanic bombs_____

Denali National Park

Where's the highest mountain in North America? Right here in Alaska! Denali (formerly known as Mt. McKinley) is so tall (20,310 feet) that its peak is nearly always covered by clouds. Walking on the tundra feels strange—it's bouncy. Don't forget to bring binoculars to spy on the grizzly bears and other wild animals.

Alaska

Find and circle these things you can see in Denali.

Arctic Warbler
Bear
Beaver
Caribou
Cliff
Cub
Dall Sheep
Fox
Glacier
Golden Eagle
Golden Plover
Grebe
Grizzly Bear
Hill
Ice
Log
Long-Tailed Jaeger
Loon
Lynx

Marmot
Moose
Mountain Goat
Mount McKinley
Otter
Pika
Ptarmigan
Raven
River
Rock
Snow Bunting
Snowshoe Hare
Spruce
Squirrel
Tern
Valley
Wheatear
Wolf
Wolverine

L	O	O	N	G	G	N	I	T	N	U	B	W	O	N	S
L	O	N	N	A	G	I	M	R	A	T	P	O	W	P	R
E	O	N	R	A	S	Q	U	I	R	R	E	L	H	E	T
Y	N	G	G	E	O	R	E	V	I	R	L	V	E	E	A
E	R	R	O	T	T	E	R	A	T	I	T	E	A	H	R
L	E	E	Y	L	A	H	K	E	H	A	R	R	T	S	C
N	L	B	E	N	D	I	E	S	O	O	M	I	E	L	T
I	G	E	L	A	P	E	L	G	D	R	N	N	A	L	I
K	A	L	L	E	V	E	N	E	M	F	E	E	R	A	C
C	E	R	A	E	C	I	U	P	D	A	F	V	V	D	W
M	N	A	V	C	A	U	C	O	L	J	R	I	A	A	A
T	E	E	F	T	I	U	R	Y	B	O	A	M	L	E	R
N	D	B	N	L	B	E	N	P	N	I	V	E	O	C	B
U	L	U	T	F	O	X	R	U	S	R	R	E	G	T	L
O	O	E	S	N	O	W	S	H	O	E	H	A	R	E	E
M	G	R	I	Z	Z	L	Y	B	E	A	R	O	C	K	R

Ever eat in a moving restaurant? There are two of them at the top of the 605-foot Space Needle. Look down on the city, then get down and explore the tide pools, astro-space displays, and more at the Pacific Science Center. Ride the monorail downtown, eat your way through Pike Place Market, then take a boat ride around Puget Sound.

Seattle

Washington

Waterfront Wonders!
See the Seattle waterfront's great scenery, sights, and shopping. Four miles long, start at either end.

7 **Waterfront Park–**
Fishing, scenery, picnicking

8 **The Seattle Aquarium–**
Dome puts you underwater for a fish-eye view

9 **Pike Street Hillclimb–**
157 steps up to fascinating...

10 **Pike Place Market–**
Longest continuously operating farmers' market in the U.S.

1 **King Street Station–**
Historic train station

2 **Klondike Gold Rush National Historical Park–**
See things needed by miners heading to the Klondike gold fields in Alaska and Canada in 1897–98

3 **Pioneer Square–**
Heart of Old Seattle; see the totem pole

4 **Washington State Ferry Terminal–**
Ferries leave for many places including Canada

5 **Seattle Harbor Tours–**
Take a tour of the harbor, Pier 55

6 **Pier 56–**
Tours to Tillicum Village at Blake Island State Park

Rogue River

Black bears, river otters, and bald eagles hunt and play along the Rogue River. Look for them as you travel this wild, watery, "road." You might choose to bounce through the tumbling water in a rubber raft. Or, would you rather roar and splash your way upstream in a jet boat?

Oregon

Backseat Bingo!

As you ride along, when you see one of these things, mark the picture square on your card. If you see a horse, mark the square with a horse on it. To play alone, pretend you are playing with a friend, and see who wins. The first filled row of squares diagonally, up and down, or across is the winner.

141

Yellowstone/Grand Teton National Parks

Wyoming

Yellowstone, the oldest national park, has Old Faithful! This famous geyser shoots water more than one hundred feet into the air. Mudpots pop and hurl their oozy contents out like little volcanoes. And hot springs spread out like spilled paint—bright blue, green, orange, and yellow. Look out for the bears!

Hot Stuff!

Do you know what to look for in Yellowstone Park? Crack the code to see!

YOZXP YVZI_____

TVBHVIH_____

YRHLM_____

NZNNLGS SLG HKIRMTH_____

TIRAAOB YVZI_____

NLLHV_____

VOP (DZKRGR)_____

ZMGVOLKV_____

YRTSLIM HSVVK_____

BVOOLDHGLMV UZOOH_____

YZOW VZTOV_____

LOW UZRGSUFO_____

KZRMG KLGH_____

YVZEVI_____

A	B	C	D	E	F	G	H	I	J	K	L	M
Z	Y	X	W	V	U	T	S	R	Q	P	O	N

N	O	P	Q	R	S	T	U	V	W	X	Y	Z
M	L	K	J	I	H	G	F	E	D	C	B	A

Grand Teton National Park

Time for some exercise! Hiking and mountain climbing are the best ways to enjoy the wild scenery of this park. Keep an eye out for moose—they're everywhere. When you're tired or just for fun, relax with a float trip on the Snake River. Or, take a boat ride around Jackson Lake. In Jackson Hole, the winter skiing is great and it is fun to watch the huge local elk herd check in for a free lunch.

Riddle Time!

What has banks, but no money?_____

What has legs, but can't walk?_____

What has eyes, but can't see?_____

What has a bed, but never sleeps?_____

What has arms, but can't hug?_____

What has hands, but can't clap?_____

What has a face, but no head?_____

What has a mouth, but never smiles?_____

What has heels, but no feet?_____

What has a head and foot, but no body?_____

What has a neck, but no head?_____

What has an elbow, but no arm?_____

What has knees, but no legs?_____

What has ears, but can't hear?_____

What has fingers, but can't type?_____

143

Glacier National Park

Want to make snowballs in summer? In this park, summer isn't just for flowers. Snow lays scattered over the ground all year. Huge rivers of ice called glaciers creep over the land, slower than a snail. Hike the trails and try to spot bighorn sheep or mountain goats before they spot you.

Montana

Stash your trash!

The national parks are our wonderful heritage. Lets keep them clean and beautiful. Draw a line from each item to its environmental lifetime.

1 month

3 months

200-500 years

Over 500 years

As much as 1,000,000 years, (maybe never!)

Lake Tahoe

Boat or "fly," sail or slide. This mountain lake is fun to visit year round. In the summer, hit the beaches for swimming, boating, or parasailing. In the winter, head for the mountain slopes surrounding Lake Tahoe. The snow is deep and the skiing is great!

California

Nevada

What Can You Do at Lake Tahoe?

Fill in the fun activities from the clues. When you finish, the letters in the boxes will tell you where you are.

__ __ ○ __   Played with a club and small ball

__ __ __ __ __ ○ __ __   Glide on an ice rink

__ ○ __   Downhill or cross-country

__ __ __ ○ __   Gallop on a horse

__ __ __ __ ○ __   You need a racket, ball, and net

__ ○ __ __   Go in a boat without a motor

__ __ ○ __   A walk in the outdoors

__ ○ __ __   Rides on the water

__ __ __ __ ○ __ __ __   Ride on the water behind a boat

Did You Know?

Lake Tahoe, a magnificent emerald-colored mountain lake located in two states, is 6,229 feet high, up to 1,640 feet deep, and 193 square miles in area.

145

Roller coaster up and down the city hills on the cable cars. Wiggle your way along Lombard Street, the most twisty street in the world. Find colorful kites for sale in Chinatown and crabs at Fisherman's Wharf. Explore gardens and an aquarium in Golden Gate Park, or the old prison on Alcatraz Island.

Did You Know?

The Golden Gate Bridge:
- is not gold but red
- has towers 746 feet high
- has a 4,200-foot main span
- is 1.7 miles long (8,981 feet)
- has main support cables 3 feet in diameter
- needs 60,000 gallons of paint to paint it

California

Hit the Road!

If you are traveling on I-80 from New York City to San Francisco, through how many states will you pass? _____

What are they? Use the map on pages 136 and 137.

_____ _____
_____ _____
_____ _____
_____ _____
_____ _____
_____

Yosemite National Park

Look up and up and up! Everything here is taller than tall. The rock cliffs and peaks push at the sky. Waterfalls look as if they are falling from the clouds. Even the trees are huge—especially the Grizzly Giant, which is a very large and tall Sequoia tree in the park.

California

All Aboard!

Yosemite is full of wonderful things to see and do. Fill in the puzzle to learn what some of them are.

Nut	Canyon
Fern	Meadow
Hike	Merced
Lake	Camping
Pass	Sequoia
Peak	Sierras
Roam	Ahwahnee
Rock	Half Dome
Tree	Mariposa
Vale	Mountain
View	Tuolumne
Eagle	Edyth Lake
Trail	El Capitan
	Yosemite Falls

Los Angeles

Los Angeles is known for Hollywood movies, the La Brea tar pits, and the historic Mexican Olvera Street market. While in L.A., you can visit a number of amusement parks as well as Griffith Park, home of the outdoor Greek Theater. And with its famous freeways, the city also has a lot of cars!

Cars, cars, and more cars!

Fill in these words that begin with C A R.

C A R __ __ __ __	A chewy treat
C A R __ __ __ __	Seeds found in rye bread
C A R __ __ __ __ __ __ __	Part of a car's engine
C A R __ __	There are 52 in a deck
C A R __ __ __ __ __	A bright red bird
C A R __ __ __ __	Watch out!
C A R __ __ __ __ __	Lots of rides and fun
C A R __ __ __ __ __	Merry-go-round
C A R __ __ __ __ __ __	He works with a hammer and nails
C A R __ __ __	A large rug
C A R __ __ __ __ __	Babies ride in style
C A R __ __ __	A rabbit's favorite food
C A R __ __ __	A cardboard box

Round and Round She Goes!

Hop aboard the ferris wheel to discover things to see in Los Angeles. The letters you need to crack the code are red.

TJOYRCDZYT   _____

FYWMM'O XRQQC   _____
    PZQB   _____

LWDDCGWWT   _____

PZQBRQ'O BZQFRM   _____

ORZ GWQDT   _____

QZYVLW DZ XQRZ MZQ _____
    UJMO   _____

LWDDCGWWT XWGD   _____

OJE PDZNO BZNJV   _____
    BWKYMZJY   _____

KYJIRQOZD OMKTJWO   _____
    LWDDCGWWT   _____

SKRRY BZQC   _____

XRIRQDC LJDDO   _____

QWOR XWGD   _____

ZPDEN TPQXPT SK   _____
    DJX ZTXEVYZG OXQD _____

YXV OMKTJWO   _____

NQJPPJML UZQF   _____
    WXORQIZMWQC   _____

MLR VWDJORKB   _____

149

Sequoia/Kings Canyon National Parks

California

Tree Ring Circus!

Some of California's trees are very big and very old. Count the rings of each of these trees to tell how old. Which two tree sections are from the same tree? Don't forget to count the middle.

You'll feel as small as an ant when you walk through the giant forest of sequoia trees (named for the Indian chief Sequoyah). The General Sherman tree is the largest living tree in the world—taller than a 25-story building. You can also see a real cabin built in a hollow log and tour Crystal Cave.

San Diego

California

In San Diego, you can have fun that's wet and wild. You can go whale watching on the ocean or hit one of the area's beaches. You can see an array of wild and endangered animals at the San Diego Safari Park or hit the city's most famous attraction: The San Diego Zoo in Balboa Park.

Do the Zoo, San Diego That Is!

Who has the longest neck?

Who has the longest nose?

Who can run the fastest?

Who is the King of the Beasts?

Who is the horse in striped pajamas?

Who can hang by his tail?

Who comes with her own pocket?

Who is called a river horse?

151

Salt Lake City

Utah

Bob like a beach ball in the Great Salt Lake. Time travel back to pioneer days with a visit to Old Deseret Village or count the organ pipes at the Mormon Tabernacle. Look for the Seagull Monument. This bird is very special to the city.

Capital Place!

How much do you know about our state capitals? Try this quiz and see!

1. What two state names are found in the names of their state capitals?

2. In which state capital is the U.S. Naval Academy located?

3. What capital name means "red stick" in French?

4. What state capital is named for our 16th president?

5. Which state capital is known as "Music City?"

6. What four states and their capitals begin with the same letter?

7. Which state capital can <u>only</u> be reached by plane or boat?

8. Name six state capitals that begin with "s."

9. Which state capital has the longest history?

10. Which state capital means "stone" in French?

Did You Know?
The Great Salt Lake is the second saltiest body of water in the world, after the Dead Sea, between 6 and 27 percent salt. Makes floating very easy!

152

Dinosaur National Monument

This park is really Jurassic! You will find more Jurassic-age dinosaur bones, skulls, and skeletons here than anywhere else in the world. There are also weird land formations caused by the wind and rain eating away at the earth. Perfect for a dinosaur park!

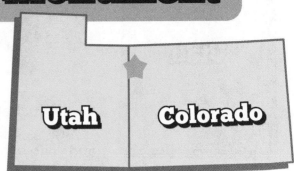

Utah　Colorado

Make No Bones About It!

At this park more than 2,000 dinosaur bones are exposed on a wall inside the park building. Can you find the six dinosaurs that are hiding outside?

Utah

Bryce Canyon/Zion National Parks

Castles, people, chessmen, a box of giant stone crayons...All kinds of strange shapes can be seen in the white, purple, pink, red, orange, and yellow rocks that fill Bryce Canyon National Park. At Zion, earn a patch from the Junior Ranger program. Also check out the hanging gardens and Weeping Rock.

Rocky Road!

These two parks have beautiful and fun things to see. Find and circle them in the puzzle below.

Bike	Hike	Sun
Bryce	Lore	Top
Camp	Red	Tower
Canyon	Ride	Wall
Cliff	Rim	Zion
Fold	Rock	

E K C L I F F
K C A M P O T
I O N W A L L
B R Y C E D O
Z I O N D E R
S U N H I K E
T O W E R I M

154

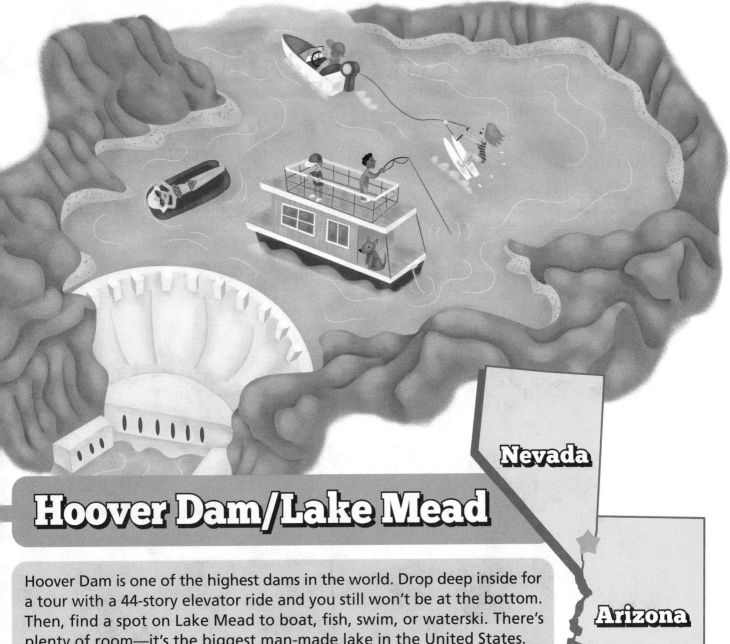

Hoover Dam/Lake Mead

Nevada

Arizona

Hoover Dam is one of the highest dams in the world. Drop deep inside for a tour with a 44-story elevator ride and you still won't be at the bottom. Then, find a spot on Lake Mead to boat, fish, swim, or waterski. There's plenty of room—it's the biggest man-made lake in the United States.

Rhyme Time!
Find the rhyming answers to each pair of riddles.

It blocks a river_____
A baby sheep_____

You walk on them_____
A large red vegetable_____

A round toy_____
Great place to shop_____

They tell the time_____
Baby toys with letters_____

It has an on/off switch_____
A dog and cat may do this_____

Finger jewelry_____
Kids like to do this_____

A smile is found on this_____
Opposite of north_____

Fun to read_____
Make dinner_____

It has two wheels_____
A walk in the woods_____

Frogs like to_____
Gasoline comes out of a_____

Grand Canyon National Park

Arizona

This is one big ditch! Stand on the South Rim of the Grand Canyon, and you'll be looking a mile down and almost 10 miles across. For a different view, look up at the massive canyon walls from a raft plunging on the Colorado River. Or, ride a mule into the canyon past the colorful, layered cliffs.

Some View!

Hop aboard a mule and ride down into the Grand Canyon. See if you can find the way.

Phoenix

Want to walk through a forest of cacti? Visit the Desert Botanical Garden where mighty saguaro cacti stand at attention like prickly crossing guards. Phoenix also has a Doll and Toy Museum, the Pueblo Grande Museum, and a Mystery Castle built of desert rocks and other found materials.

Arizona

Prickly Place!

Deserts have beautiful cacti, wildflower, and desert plants. Color these that are found in Arizona. Saguaro's big arms have white and yellow flowers. Pink flowers crown the short, round, gray-green pincushion. Bear grass is bushy with a tall white flower. Red blossoms tip the ocotillo's long, thin branches. Prickly pear has flat, thick leaves with golden flowers. Orange blooms top the barrel cactus. Joshua tree branches have green, prickly, bushy ends. Hedgehog has dark pink blossoms.

157

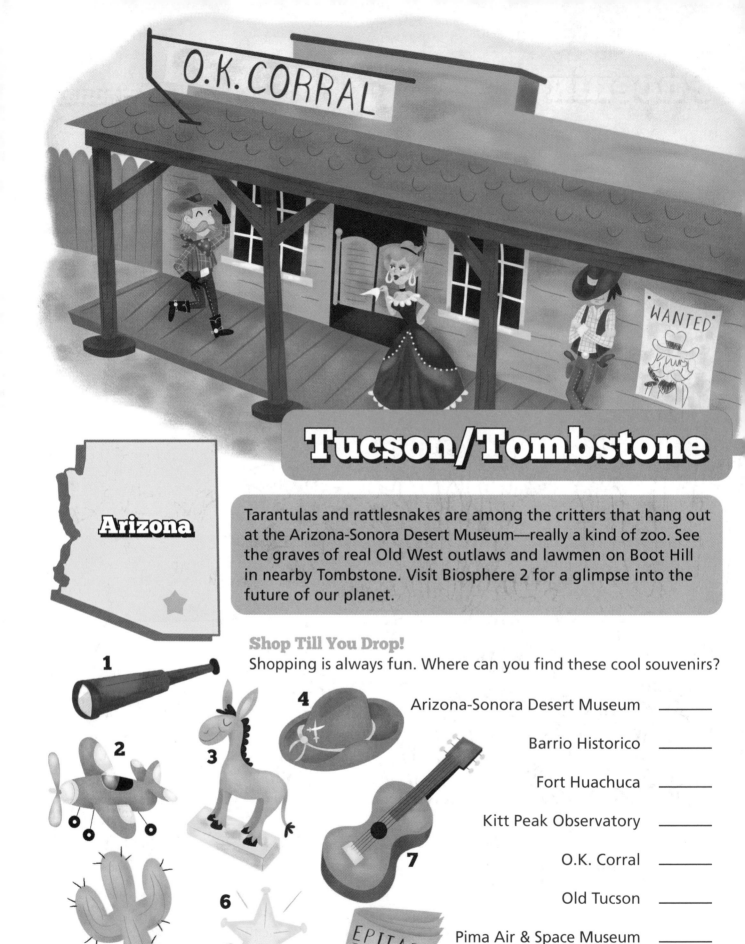

O.K. CORRAL

Tucson/Tombstone

Arizona

Tarantulas and rattlesnakes are among the critters that hang out at the Arizona-Sonora Desert Museum—really a kind of zoo. See the graves of real Old West outlaws and lawmen on Boot Hill in nearby Tombstone. Visit Biosphere 2 for a glimpse into the future of our planet.

Shop Till You Drop!
Shopping is always fun. Where can you find these cool souvenirs?

Arizona-Sonora Desert Museum _____

Barrio Historico _____

Fort Huachuca _____

Kitt Peak Observatory _____

O.K. Corral _____

Old Tucson _____

Pima Air & Space Museum _____

Tombstone _____

WANTED

EPITAPH

Santa Fe/Taos

In Santa Fe, hurry over to the Museum of International Folk Art to see a huge display of folk art, toys, and miniatures. You can learn about the people of the southwest at the Museum of Indian Arts and Culture or get in on the action at the Children's Museum. Then venture 70 miles north to Taos to visit ancient pueblo dwellings.

New Mexico

Ancient Apartment House!
Use your imagination and color the pueblo below.

Mesa Verde National Park

Mesa Verde means "green table" in Spanish, and that's just what this huge, forest-covered rock platform looks like. But it's a table with a secret. From the top, peer down at the ancient cliff dwellings of the Ancestral Puebloan culture. A golden stone city waiting to be explored.

Pick a Path!
Start up the ladder and wind your way through the ruins on one of the two paths that lead to Balcony House or follow another path to the Kiva.

Colorado

KIVA

BALCONY HOUSE

Denver/Colorado Springs

Start your Colorado adventure in Denver with a visit to the U.S. Mint, where billions of coins are made every year. Then head south to Colorado Springs, where you can drive, bike, or hike to the top of Pikes Peak. And in winter, don't forget skiing at the many resorts in the Rocky Mountains!

Colorado

Awesome!
Find the right ski trail to the bottom of Pikes Peak.

LODGE

Oklahoma City/Tulsa

In Oklahoma City, visit the capitol building which has several working oil wells within a half mile. Then check out the National Cowboy Museum where you can dress up as a cowpoke and experience a real old-west town. In Tulsa, stand at the "Center of the Universe" and create an echo only you can hear. Then head out to the one of many ranches and go horseback riding.

Sooner State Fun!
Unscramble the words to spell out the name of something you can see or do in Oklahoma!

OOBCYW _____

LOI LEWL _____

PACLIOT DNUGIBLI _____

HANRECS _____

DOL TWSE _____

LEEGCRISA UUMSME _____

SHOERS _____

HOEC _____

Did You Know?

In Tulsa, the Gilcrease Museum, one of the world's finest American West art and artifact collections, was founded by Thomas Gilcrease, a citizen of the Muscogee Creek Nation, who made his fortune in oil.

Dallas/Fort Worth

Attend a western rodeo and cheer on real-life cowboys and cowgirls. Investigate pioneer life at the Dallas Heritage Village or Log Cabin Village in Fort Worth. The days of cattle drives come alive at the Fort Worth Stockyards National Historic District. And for modern-day excitement, there are many sporting options in the area.

Texas

Catch This!
For one minute, study these 10 items you use to play sports. Close the book and see if you can remember all 10.

163

Explore by foot...or by boat! A river runs right through downtown. Downtown is also where you'll find that famous Spanish mission (and battle site) the Alamo, Historic Market Square, and lots of great museums. When you need a history break, cheer on the watery stars at SeaWorld of San Antonio.

San Antonio

Texas

Buena Suerte!

San Antonio has lots of Spanish atmosphere. Identify these Spanish words from the scene below.

arbol ____   burro ____   casa ____   gato ____   iglesia ____   mano ____

niña ____   niño ____   pelo ____   pelota ____   perro ____   piñata ____

serape ____   sol ____   sombrero ____   zapatos ____

Minneapolis/St. Paul

Minnesota

Don't worry about cold weather in the winter: Glass skyways connect downtown buildings – a hamster maze for humans! In the summer, you can swim and fish in the area's many lakes. Or, hop aboard for a paddlewheel boat ride on the Mississippi River. And don't forget to check out the Minneapolis Sculpture Garden with its famous giant spoon and cherry.

Cruisin' Down the River!

If you were Tom Sawyer or Huck Finn floating down the Mississippi River on a raft, what states would you pass on your travels?

Start at the arrow and write every other letter until you have gone around the circle twice, filling in the blanks.

M _ _ _ _ _ _ _ _ _ _ _ _ _ _

I _ _ _ _

M _ _ _ _ _ _ _

A _ _ _ _ _ _ _

L _ _ _ _ _ _ _ _

W _ _ _ _ _ _ _ _ _

I _ _ _ _ _ _ _

K _ _ _ _ _ _ _

T _ _ _ _ _ _ _ _

M _ _ _ _ _ _ _ _ _ _ _

Black Hills

South Dakota

This is gold country! Grab a pan and sift for nuggets like an old-time prospector, or tour a mine. Haunt a ghost town, or prowl caves filled with jewel-like crystals. Chug the tracks in an 1880 steam train. At Mt. Rushmore you'll see presidents with noses almost as long as a school bus!

Gold Mining!
Find the six hidden things about the Black Hills.

Scenic Stumpers!

How about a game to help you enjoy the scenery? Can be played with several people or alone.

1. The first player picks something from the passing scene.

2. The next person has to name something that begins with the last letter of the first item.

3. Try to stump the other players by picking something with an unusual last letter (for example "X").

4. If all are stumped by your word, you get to start the next game.

Black Hills Trivia

- Gold comes in many different colors.
- The heads on Mt. Rushmore are 60 feet from forehead to chin and took 14 years to carve.
- There are many beautiful caves to visit beneath the Black Hills.
- Bison bulls weigh nearly a ton and can run faster than a horse.
- Custer State Park has many bison and some famous begging burros.
- You can still pan for gold today in the Black Hills.
- Wooly mammoths once lived around Hot Springs in the Black Hills.

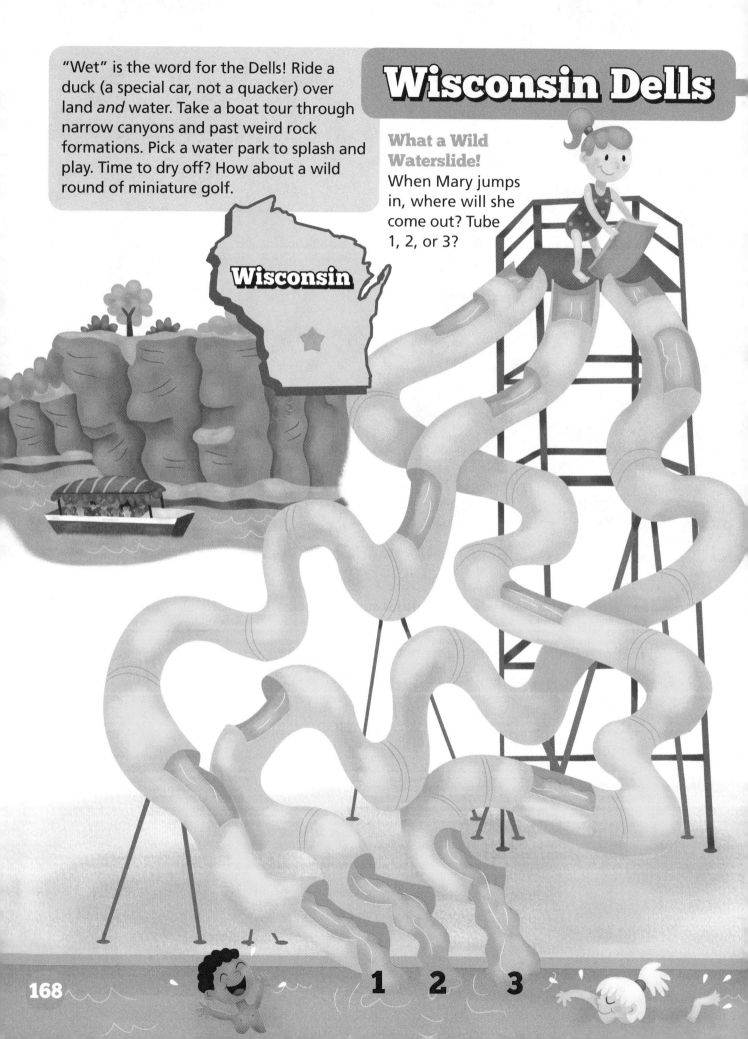

"Wet" is the word for the Dells! Ride a duck (a special car, not a quacker) over land *and* water. Take a boat tour through narrow canyons and past weird rock formations. Pick a water park to splash and play. Time to dry off? How about a wild round of miniature golf.

Wisconsin Dells

Wisconsin

What a Wild Waterslide!

When Mary jumps in, where will she come out? Tube 1, 2, or 3?

1 2 3

Milwaukee

Walk through a rain forest or meet face-to-face with life-size dinosaurs at the Milwaukee Public Museum. Then, experiment with science at Discovery World. After a stop at the terrific zoo, wander through the Domes. These round plant museums are HUGE! Each is almost half a foodball field wide and seven stories tall.

Whose lunch?

Lunches got all mixed up at the zoo. Help each animal find its own lunch. Draw a line to join the right pairs.

For an eagle's-eye view of the city, soar to the top of Willis Tower—Chicago's tallest building. Watch whales at the Shedd Aquarium, climb through a coal mine at the Museum of Science and Industry, or enter an Egyptian tomb at the Field Museum. Then, go ape with the gorillas at Lincoln Park Zoo.

Chicago

Illinois

Great Shape!
If you try, you can see other shapes in several of the Great Lakes. Identify the lakes that have shapes like these.

LAKE SUPERIOR

MICH.

WISCONSIN

LAKE MICHIGAN

LAKE HURON

MICHIGAN

CANADA

LAKE ONTARIO

NEW YORK

LAKE ERIE

PENNSYLVANIA

ILLINOIS

INDIANA

OHIO

Did You Know?
Combine the first letters of the names of the Great Lakes to spell HOMES. It will help you remember them (Huron, Ontario, Michigan, Erie, Superior).

Dearborn

Michigan

American sights and sounds fill the Henry Ford Museum. Build a Model T, see a massive toy train display, and step inside the bus Rosa Parks made history in. Next stop is the Greenfield Village, where you can visit such places as the Wright brothers' shop, Thomas Edison's laboratory, or ride on an antique carousel.

Alphabet Favorites!
Wow! Look at all of these cool things. Can you find something that begins with each letter of the alphabet.

BE MINE

In the world's largest Children's Museum you can explore a cave, match wits with computers, and conduct scientific experiments. Or, "drive" a real Indy 500 car, whirl on a carousel, and zoom through deep space.

Indianapolis

Indiana

Race Away!

You will need three different coins to play this game—two to use as markers and one to flip. Flip the coin to determine how many spaces to move—heads, move two spaces; tails move one space. Follow the directions on spaces where you land. First one to the Finish Line takes the checkered flag.

START

FINISH

LAP LEADER MOVE 3 SPACES

SPIN OUT MOVE 1 SPACE BACK

GREEN FLAG MOVE 3 SPACES

CAUTION MOVE 1 SPACE

OUT OF GAS LOSE 1 TURN

NEW TIRES EXTRA TURN

DEBRIS ON TRACK MOVE 1 SPACE BACK

FLAT TIRE MOVE 2 SPACES BACK

HIT THE WALL! YOU LOSE

PIT STOP LOSE 1 TURN

Bluegrass Country

Kentucky

Like horses? You'll LOVE Kentucky Horse Park in Lexington. There are all kinds of horsey things to see and do. For horse racing excitement, ride over to the Kentucky Derby Museum in Louisville. Or, take a sternwheeler cruise, learn "The Legend of Daniel Boone," explore a fort, or see Lincoln's birthplace.

Horses, Horses, Horses!
Can you correctly identify these parts of a horse? Fill in the numbers.

Barrel_____   Hoof_____

Chest_____   Mane_____

Fetlock_____   Nostrils_____

Forelock_____   Tail_____

Haunch_____   Thigh_____

Hock_____   Withers_____

How much do you know about horses? True or False?

A newborn horse is a foal._____

A mare is a mother horse._____

All Thoroughbred horses are one year older every January 1st. _____

Horses always sleep lying down._____

Horses were brought to America by the Spaniards. _____

The father of a horse is its sire._____

Ponies are baby horses._____

Mammoth Cave National Park

Go back in time and visit an assortment of "stone age" things such as a waterfall, icicles, popcorn, snowballs, and flowers. Special sections include Fat Man's Misery, Bottomless Pit, and Mummy Ledge. Oh, don't forget a jacket—caves are really "cool" places.

Kentucky

Black Hills Trivia

Stalagmites grow up, while stalactites grow down.

Did you know that many fish in caves are either blind or have no eyes at all?

Caves are formed in limestone rocks by dripping or running water.

Mammoth Cave has more than 330 miles of explored passageways, and it is still growing.

The Snowball Dining Room is 267 feet beneath the surface.

The temperature in the cave is 54°F all year.

Mammoth Cave is the longest known cave system in the world, and there are many other caves in the area.

Bats are in some caves, but they often leave at sundown to eat.

St. Louis

Scrunch into an elevator that looks kind of like a clothes dryer, and ride up Gateway Arch to see the sights. Back on the ground, find everything from furry-footed Clydesdale horses to bison at Grants Farm. Catch your shadow at the Magic House, or roam the zoo and Science Center in Forest Park.

Scrambled States!

It would be fun to visit some of the cool places in this book. Unscramble the states and write the correct name next to the mixed-up letters. Then next to the landmark places, write the correct number for the matching state.

Missouri

State

1. FLAIRCOINA _____

2. RISOSUMI _____

3. WEN KORY _____

4. DOOLACOR _____

5. LISINILO _____

6. EWN OCXIEM _____

7. VENSILPANNAY _____

8. ESENETNSE _____

9. IIAVNGIR _____

10. CD SNAOGWTHNI _____

Landmark

Pueblos _____

Statue of Liberty _____

Grand Ole Opry _____

Lincoln Memorial_____

Hollywood_____

Colonial Williamsburg _____

Field Museum _____

Gateway Arch_____

Liberty Bell _____

Pikes Peak_____

175

Skinny, twisting roads roller coaster the Ozark Mountains. At the Ozark Folk Center, see what mountain life was like before there were roads. Spend a day at Silver Dollar City. Ride the rides, listen to country music, watch old-time crafters or tour a cave. Fish and swim at Table Rock Lake, or catch the shows in Branson.

Fun Time!

Find and circle these things you can see and do on vacation. Then find the secret message in the leftover letters.

Missouri

Arkansas

Ozarks

Ball	Merry-go-round
Bike	Museum
Boat	Raft
Bumper cars	Read
Camp	Ride
Cave	Roller coaster
Climb	Row
Drive	Sail
Eat	Sand castles
Ferry	Shop
Fish	Sightsee
Fly	Ski
Golf	Sled
Green	Sleep
Hike	Sports
Horse	Swim
Inner tube	Swing
Lake	Trip
Limbo	Water park
Look	Zoo

R	O	W	S	R	A	C	R	E	P	M	U	B
A	O	F	A	E	A	T	M	G	N	I	W	S
F	T	L	I	A	H	A	E	Y	L	F	E	E
T	A	O	L	D	S	T	R	O	P	S	E	L
E	O	G	R	E	E	N	R	V	I	K	S	T
Z	B	E	F	E	R	R	Y	I	I	R	T	S
A	M	U	K	I	I	C	G	B	P	A	H	A
M	I	A	T	D	S	G	O	P	O	P	G	C
U	L	O	E	R	D	H	R	A	E	R	I	D
E	C	O	L	V	E	H	O	R	S	E	S	N
S	A	A	O	L	I	N	U	P	W	T	L	A
U	V	T	M	K	A	R	N	I	I	A	E	S
M	E	M	E	P	E	B	D	I	M	W	D	R

Natchez

Clip-clop through town in a horse-drawn carriage as they did in the old days. Visit the Grand Village of the Natchez Indians and see a Native American house. Along the Natchez Trace Parkway, you will find an eerie cypress swamp.

Mississippi

Shapely States!

Many states are shaped like no other state. Can you identify these states just from their shape? Check the map on pages 136 and 137, if you need a hint.

Clap to the music of street performers in the French Quarter. See the Mississippi from a sternwheeler or a ferry. Meet some "finny friends" at the aquarium, or hop on a bell-clanging streetcar to the fabulous zoo. Boat the lagoons, ride the carousel, or visit Storyland in City Park.

New Orleans

Louisiana

Sail Away!

Down the Mississippi River sail two identical sternwheelers—or are they? Can you find 10 differences between them?

Huntsville

Alabama

Feeling spacey? Head for the U.S. Space and Rocket Center. You can take a bus tour of the NASA labs and shuttle test sites. Try out weightlessness, work hands-on displays, or surround yourself with an Omnimax space exploration film. An outdoor park is filled with a forest of real rockets.

Off to Space!

Rockets sprout like tulips in this rocket park. Follow-the-dots to add a few more, then color the picture.

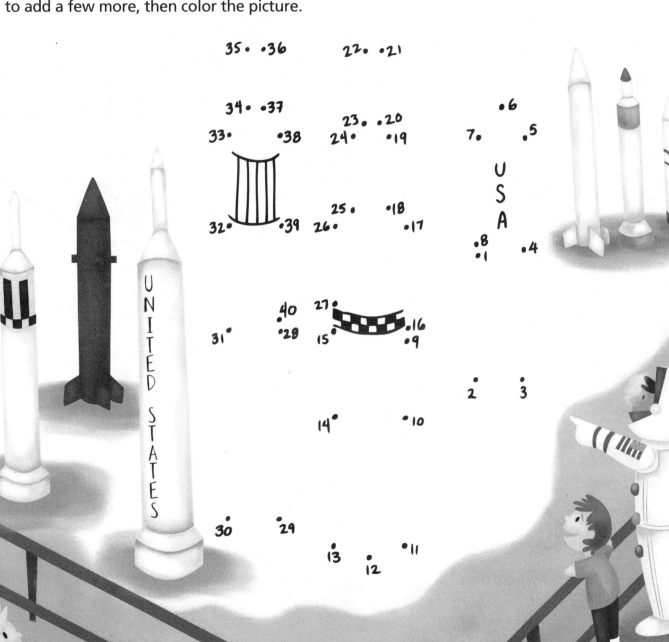

Nashville moves to the beat of country music. Hear its sounds at the Grand Ole Opry and take a tour backstage! To experience the life of the city's first settlers, visit Fort Nashborough, perched along the banks of the Cumberland River. For outdoor fun – go boating, fishing, or hiking at Percy Priest Lake.

Nashville

Tennessee

Music City!

Study these musical instruments for one minute.
Close the book and see how many you can remember.

Great Smoky Mountains National Park

Tennessee ★ North Carolina

Pull on your hiking boots and hit the trail—the Appalachian Trail. It snakes through the park high along the crest of the mountains. There are lots of shorter trails, too. See the mountain villages in the valleys hidden by bluish mist? That's the "smoke" in Great Smoky. You can camp overnight and explore the Blue Ridge Parkway in the area.

Hit the Road!

The kids ran because their trip was starting. Add one letter to the letters on the first line, scramble them to form a new word. Repeat on each line. Each new word must contain all of the letters of the word above it. Hint—subtract R, A, and N from STARTING to see what letters to use.

R A N

S T A R T I N G

What's in a Name?

How many words are hiding in the name
GREAT SMOKY MOUNTAINS
(100, maybe 200! No plurals, no proper names)?

Visit the Center for Puppetry Arts to learn about and be entertained by puppets from around the world. At the Cyclorama, see and hear a Civil War battle come alive as you sit inside a huge, round painting. Check out the Martin Luther King, Jr. National Historical Park to see the home where Dr. King was born. Or, take one of many train rides in the area to complete your visit.

Atlanta

Georgia

Lots to see!
Build this pyramid with names of things to see in Atlanta. Each name must fill a complete row of squares and no more.

BRAVES

CAPITOL

CNN

CYCLORAMA

MARTA

M.L. KING SITE

OMNI

SIX FLAGS

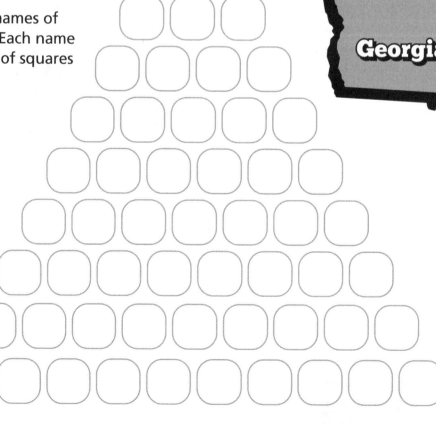

Tampa/St. Petersburg

Take a safari and get a close-up look at giraffes, zebras, and rhinos at Busch Gardens. Out on the St. Pete Pier, you can fish, eat, and visit an aquarium. Feel like building a sand castle or body-surfing some waves? Grab a shovel and a suit, then head for St. Pete's beaches.

Florida

Ahoy Matey!
Shiver me timbers, where's my ship? Connect the dots in order, then color the picture.

Central Florida/Orlando

Florida

Central Florida is theme park heaven! Visit the area's parks and you can travel the world, see how movie stunts are created, and get to know whales and sharks up close! When you're done splashing in the pool, there are roller coasters to ride, animals to see, and even gravity defying waterski shows to view.

What's Up!

What can you find in Central Florida? Solve the sentences below, then fill the right letters in the matching slots at the bottom.

1. Find me in light and toy _____
2. Find me in horse and hug _____
3. Find me in car and ride _____
4. Find me in ice and big _____
5. Find me in log and pile _____
6. Find me in line and luck _____
7. Find me in smile and sad _____

Did You Know?

Central Florida is a fun-filled playground today. Not too long ago it was mostly acres and acres of citrus groves, large cattle ranches, and a few swamps.

I spy!

If you're looking out the window, try to find something that begins with each letter of the alphabet, in order. You can play this game alone or with another traveler.

___ ___ ___ ___ ___ ___ ___
 1   2   3   4   5   6   7

BOAT TOURS

ACTION

Nonstop Fun!

Unscramble the words below to spell out the name of something you can see or do in Central Florida!

AKRHS _____

LOLRRE TROSEAC _____

TRAAOBI _____

RTAKWIES _____

ONDHILSP _____

EVMIO TTSNU _____

OLAONBL _____

TROALALGI _____

STEALC _____

SHEABEC _____

Central Florida

Want more? Ride a glass-bottom boat over rainbow-colored fish. Find your state stone in a monument built of cement and stones from every state. Take an airboat ride and if you're lucky enough, you may see some alligators in the wild!

Everglades National Park

Board an airboat and skim over this "river of grass." Keep a watch out for wildlife. Birds come in many colors—red, blue, pink, white, yellow, and green. Long-legged herons stalk for fish. Alligators and crocodiles lie like floating logs. You may glimpse a shy sea cow (manatee), or see a slithery snake.

Florida

Snakes, pelicans, and gators, oh my!
Can you solve these rebus puzzles about things to see in the Everglades?

GAL. − G + 👁 + 🏯 + ✕

🥄 + YOU OWE $10.00

👧 − H + 🎀 + T

🪚 + 〰

C + 🌧 ←

T + 👗 ↙ − SK + L

S N + 🧹 − R

Cape Canaveral/Titusville

Florida

This is where the space shuttles lift off. Start at the Kennedy Space Center to experience the blast of an imitation countdown and launch—maybe even a real one! See space capsules and space suits. And, hundreds of birds who share their sky with man.

Cape Caper!
Strange things are happening at Cape Canaveral and Merritt Island National Wildlife Refuge. Find nine things that are not quite right.

St. Augustine

Florida

This city is OLD – the oldest in the United States. Cross the moat and climb the ramparts of a 300-year-old fort. Wander the narrow streets to find the oldest house and the oldest wood school. Stop for a sip at the Fountain of Youth or a dip at the beach.

Aaaarrrgggghhhh!

St. Augustine has a long history with pirates, and even has a Pirate and Treasure Museum. Find and circle the pirate words in the puzzle.

Pirate	Loot
Treasure	Gold
Blackbeard	Bounty
Booty	Chest
Aye	Ahoy
Buccaneer	Ship
Plank	Blimey
Telescope	

B	L	A	C	K	B	E	A	R	D	T	O	H	O
O	E	B	E	Y	O	K	O	P	I	R	A	T	E
B	T	A	Y	B	N	E	T	R	H	B	O	R	O
P	L	L	A	A	R	T	L	E	I	E	B	L	R
T	H	I	L	N	E	A	B	B	C	H	C	P	I
E	T	P	M	S	A	O	O	T	C	N	I	L	L
R	O	B	T	E	D	O	H	Y	A	H	O	Y	A
U	O	O	R	E	Y	A	T	O	S	R	E	H	T
S	L	B	O	U	N	T	Y	S	T	R	K	C	O
A	L	D	S	A	L	E	P	B	E	A	O	B	L
E	B	U	C	C	A	N	E	E	R	H	L	O	G
R	Y	E	P	O	C	S	E	L	E	T	C	O	O
T	C	Y	L	A	E	O	H	E	P	Y	L	T	C
O	L	K	C	E	A	A	B	T	S	D	U	Y	T

Charleston

Explore a five-sided piece of American history, Fort Sumter, where the first shots of the Civil War were fired. At Charles Towne Landing, see a colonial village, sailing ships, wolves, bears, pumas, and other native wildlife roaming the Animal Forest.

Spot These Sights!

Play Tic-Tac-Toe with Charleston sights. Look for the item (or something sort of like it) pictured in the square you want to play. When you find it put a coin or marker over the picture. Set a limit on how long you can look for the correct item. Each player should use a different type of coin or marker. If you are playing alone, see how long it takes you to get three in a row, or to cover the whole board.

Bridge	Garden	Church
Theater	Fort Sumter	Golf Course
Boat	House	Horse and Buggy

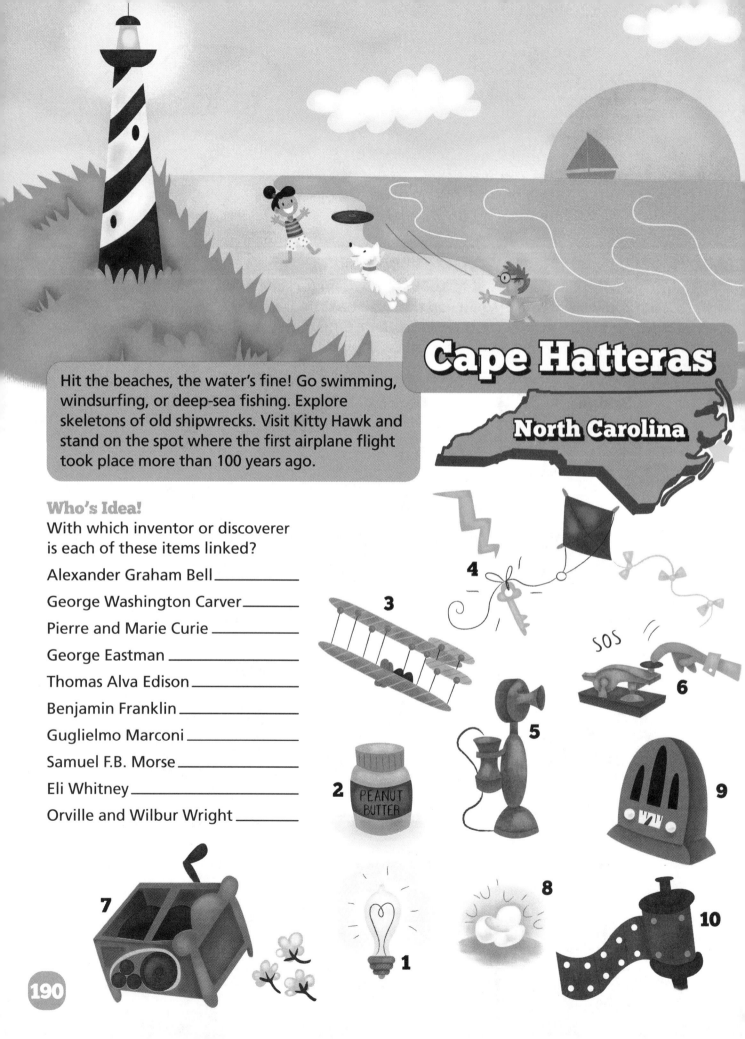

Cape Hatteras
North Carolina

Hit the beaches, the water's fine! Go swimming, windsurfing, or deep-sea fishing. Explore skeletons of old shipwrecks. Visit Kitty Hawk and stand on the spot where the first airplane flight took place more than 100 years ago.

Who's Idea!

With which inventor or discoverer is each of these items linked?

Alexander Graham Bell _____

George Washington Carver _____

Pierre and Marie Curie _____

George Eastman _____

Thomas Alva Edison _____

Benjamin Franklin _____

Guglielmo Marconi _____

Samuel F.B. Morse _____

Eli Whitney _____

Orville and Wilbur Wright _____

Williamsburg

Virginia

Go back in time at Colonial Williamsburg – back to the 18th Century. In the shops, wigs and perukes are made, barrels are shaped, and teapots are carefully crafted out of fine sliver. A wooden stock sits, ready to lock in those who misbehave, while men in waistcoats greet women in hoop-skirted dresses. Take a carriage ride, learn to prepare an authentic colonial meal, and don't forget to watch the march of the Fifes and Drums.

You Make What?

Match the historic names of these tradesmen with the items they made. Fill in the proper number after its matching trade.

Apothecary _____

Baker _____

Blacksmith _____

Cabinetmaker _____

Cooper _____

Milliner _____

Peruke Maker _____

Silversmith _____

Wheelwright _____

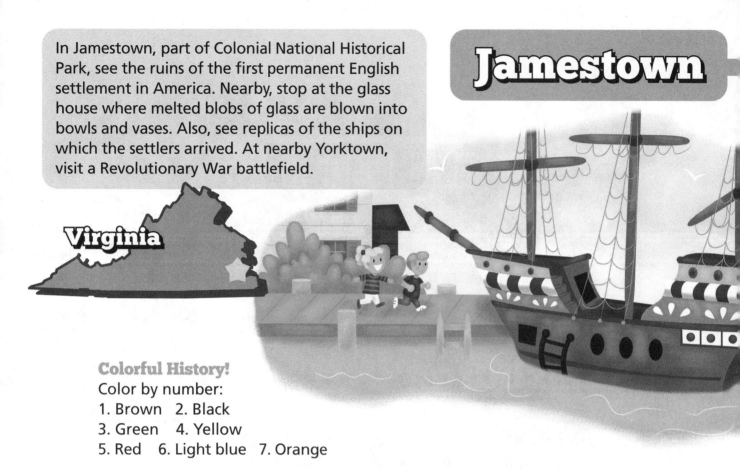

In Jamestown, part of Colonial National Historical Park, see the ruins of the first permanent English settlement in America. Nearby, stop at the glass house where melted blobs of glass are blown into bowls and vases. Also, see replicas of the ships on which the settlers arrived. At nearby Yorktown, visit a Revolutionary War battlefield.

Jamestown

Virginia

Colorful History!
Color by number:
1. Brown   2. Black
3. Green   4. Yellow
5. Red   6. Light blue   7. Orange

Baltimore

Maryland

Rustle through a rain forest, stare down a shark, beware of the red-bellied piranha when you enter the National Aquarium. Climb aboard a ship that battled pirates almost 200 years ago. Visit Babe Ruth's birthplace and Ft. McHenry—the site of the battle that inspired the "Star Spangled Banner."

Fancy Fins!

See all of the beautiful fish. Only two of them are alike. Can you find them?

Washington, D.C.

You'll love visiting the nation's capital for its hands-on museums and plentiful attractions. Stroll the 2-mile National Mall from the Lincoln Memorial to the U.S. Capitol. At the city's many museums you can view former President Theodore Roosevelt's teddy bear, touch a rock from the moon, and see the Wright Brothers' plane.

Oh Say Can You See in Washington, D.C.?
Fill in the sights.

Museums:
Freer
Smithsonian
U.S. Holocaust

Memorials:
Jefferson
Lincoln
Vietnam Veterans
(The) Wall

Capitol
Congress
FBI
Ford's Theater
Kennedy Center
Mall
Potomac (River)
Supreme Court
Union (Station)
Washington Monument
White House
Wolf Trap
Zoo

Capital Quiz!

How much do you know about our nation's capital? Try this quiz and see.

What is the tallest stone structure in the world?

Where do they print money?

What monument has more than 58,000 names on it?

Where can you find the Wright Brothers' 1903 *Flyer*, Lindbergh's *Spirit of St. Louis*, and the *Apollo* command module?

Where does the president live?

What is found on the land surrounding Robert E. Lee's former home?

What is the "Castle?"

Where can you see a panda?

Pittsburgh
Pennsylvania

Downtown sits in a "Golden Triangle." Rivers sweep by two sides to form the Ohio River at the triangle's point. Creep steeply up Mount Washington by incline (hill-climbing trolleys) for a great view of all three rivers. Control your own sky trip at the Science Center. Roam Dinosaur Hall at the Natural History Museum.

Solve the Mystery!

How many triangles are hidden in this mysterious pyramid? How many can you find?

Secret clue...some are made up of more than one little triangle!

Did You Know?

Pittsburgh is known as the "city of bridges" because it has 446 bridges—more than any other city in the world.

Lancaster

Pennsylvania

Enter the world of the Amish. Children study in one-room schools. Men have beards and women wear bonnets. See mule-drawn plows and horse-drawn buggies (even ride in one), but no electric lights—or TV! Nearby Hershey has chocolate air, kiss-shaped streetlights, and a fascinating theme park.

Plain or Fancy?

Many Amish people often do not use modern or fancy things. Draw a line to those they would use. Which would they not use?

Philadelphia

Pennsylvania

The early capital of the United States, Philadelphia is filled with attractions. Visit Independence Hall and see the Liberty Bell. At Penn's Landing, board a battleship or squeeze into a submarine. The Franklin Institute features all sorts of hands-on science and technology experiments while America's first zoo has a large climbing structure for monkeys – and one just for kids!

Did You Know?

Philly is famous for...
The Liberty Bell (a must-see for everyone)
Hot pretzels (with or without mustard) sold by corner vendors
Cheesesteak sandwiches (a tasty treat)

Did You Know That?

Philadelphia was the home of many famous firsts.

The first U.S. flag, with 13 stars and 13 stripes, was made in Philadelphia. Tradition says, by Betsy Ross.

The first U.S. zoo

The first Bank of the United States

The first stock exchange

The first fire-fighting company

The first U.S. mint to coin money

The first daily newspaper

The first bifocal glasses, invented by Ben Franklin

The first public library

The first root beer, invented by Charles Hires

The first ice cream soda

The first motion picture show in the world

The first public demonstration of the telephone

Can You Come Out Even?

As you follow around the square, add and subtract, as directed, the number related to each item listed in the little squares. See if you can come out with the same totals as given at two of the corners.

→ **=1** **+ Goldilock's Bears** **=** **+ Major Oceans (Seas)** **=** **− Fingers** **=** **+ Planets** **=**

− Corners in a square **− Quintet**

= **=**

− Age to vote **+ U.S. States**

= **=**

− Original Colonies **− Dozen**

= **=**

+ Bakers Dozen **− Stripes in U.S. Flag**

= **+ Pair** **=** **− Half Dozen** **=** **+ Lucky Clover Leaves** **=** **− Continents** **30 =**

Valley Forge
Pennsylvania

Gaze out over the beautiful rolling green hills of this national historical park, and try to imagine you're a soldier in the winter of 1777. It is arctic cold. You're hungry and sick. The tiny log hut you share with other soldiers is bare and dark. General Washington makes battle plans in the stone house that is his headquarters. Life was hard at Valley Forge.

Silent Sentinels!
Antique cannons sit silently, reminding us of the hard-fought American Revolution, when we won our freedom. Two are alike. Find them.

Niagara Falls

These falls are part American and part Canadian. Peer down on them from a tower almost 300 feet high. For a closer view, head for the island at the edge of the plunging water. For a REALLY close look (you'll get wet) take a boat ride past the base of the falls, or walk right into the spray.

Awesome!
Guide *The Maid of the Mist* safely through the thundering waters back to the pier.

The Statue of Liberty and Brooklyn Bridge are only a couple of the famous landmarks in America's most populated city. Chug past the sights on a ferry. Buy a hot dog from a street vendor. Don't miss the zoo and carousel in Central Park, the Natural History Museum, and the Intrepid Sea, Air & Space Museum, or the ships at South Street Seaport.

New York

New York

Did You Know?

More than 12 million immigrants entered the United States through Ellis Island between 1892 and 1954. The one-day record 12,000 people on April 17, 1907. Today Ellis Island is part of the Statue of Liberty National Monument.

Build Your Own Skyscraper!
How many blocks are in this stack? There are no hidden spaces. Sort of looks like a skyscraper, doesn't it?

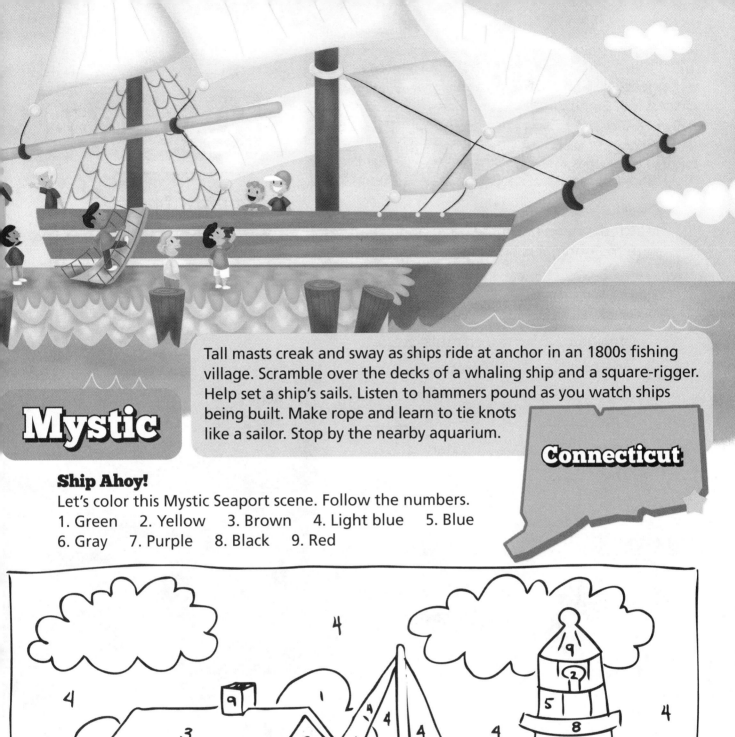

Mystic

Tall masts creak and sway as ships ride at anchor in an 1800s fishing village. Scramble over the decks of a whaling ship and a square-rigger. Help set a ship's sails. Listen to hammers pound as you watch ships being built. Make rope and learn to tie knots like a sailor. Stop by the nearby aquarium.

Connecticut

Ship Ahoy!

Let's color this Mystic Seaport scene. Follow the numbers.

1. Green   2. Yellow   3. Brown   4. Light blue   5. Blue
6. Gray   7. Purple   8. Black   9. Red

Climb sand dunes and race small shore birds along the beaches. Swim, boat, go fishing, or go whale watching. Climb Pilgrim Monument tower. Like to bike? There are great bike trails all over Cape Cod. Or, ferry out to Martha's Vineyard or Nantucket for two-wheel island exploring.

Cape Cod
Massachusetts

Chart Challenge!

Match the names of these geographic features with their numbers on the map.

Bay _____   Lake _____

Canal _____   Ocean _____

Cape _____   Peninsula _____

Channel _____   Reservoir _____

Dam _____   River _____

Delta _____   Sound _____

Inlet _____   Tributary _____

Island _____

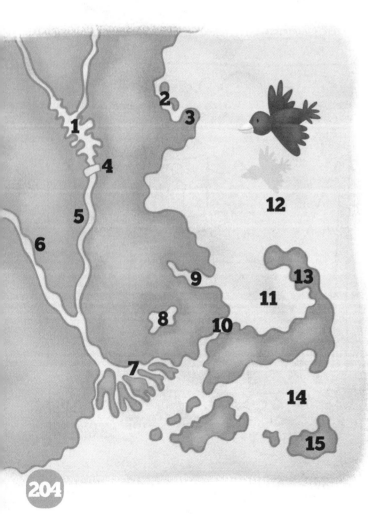

Plymouth

Massachusetts

See Plymouth Rock where the Pilgrims landed in 1620, and explore the small, crowded quarters of a replica of their ship, the *Mayflower*. At Plimoth Plantation, the Pilgrims will take time to chat with you as they go about their daily chores—cooking, mending a roof, gardening, or tending the livestock.

Decode It!

Crack the code to solve these Plymouth sights.

A = ◆	N = ✿
B = ✳	O = ↑
C = ✓	P = ▼
D = △	Q = ☽
E = ◇	R = ☆
F = ✕	S = □
G = ■	T = ▲
H = ○	U = ↓
I = ✴	V = ❖
J = ●	W = ✧
K = ✚	X = ✦
L = ▽	Y = →
M = ⌘	Z = ←

▼▽✴⌘↑▲○   ▼▽◆✿▲◆▲✴↑✿

_____

⌘◆→✕▽↑✧◇☆

_____

▼▽→⌘↑↓▲○   ☆↑✓✚

_____

▼✴▽■☆✴⌘   ❖✴▽▽◆■◇

_____

✕↑☆◇✕◆▲○◇☆□   ⌘↑✿↓⌘◇✿▲

_____

⌘→▽◇□   □▲◆◆✿△✴□○   ⌘↑✿↓⌘◇✿▲

_____

▼✴▽■☆✴⌘   ○◆▼▽▽   ⌘↓□◇↓⌘

_____

↑▽△   ✕↑☆▲   ○↑↓□◇

_____

Look down at the map and find the numbers...then walk your way through history. Peek into Paul Revere's house, visit John Hancock's grave, tread the decks of "Old Ironsides." Visit the four-story aquarium, ride a swan boat, or eat at the Quincy Market food stalls.

Boston

Massachusetts

Follow the Freedom Trail!
The green brick line leads to history. The trail is 3 miles long. Here are the highlights.

❶ **Begin at Boston Common–**
Oldest U.S. public park

❷ **State House and Archives (1795)**

❸ **Park Street Church (1809)**
Gun powder factory, War of 1812

❹ **Granary Burying Ground**
John Hancock, Samuel Adams, and Paul Revere are buried here

❺ **King's Chapel (1754)**

❻ **First Public School Site (1635)**
and Benjamin Franklin statue

❼ **Old Corner Bookstore (1712)**
Famous authors met here

❽ **Old South Meeting House (1729)**
Boston Tea Party began here

❾ **Old State House (1713)**
Now Museum of Boston History

❿ **Boston Massacre Site**
British soldiers fought colonists

⓫ **Faneuil Hall (1742)**
Called "the Cradle of Liberty"

⓬ **Paul Revere House (ca. 1680)**
Oldest Structure in Boston

⓭ **Old North Church-Christ Church (1723)**
City's oldest church still in use. In April 1775, lanterns in the steeple warned of the British coming—one if by land; two if by sea

⓮ **Copp's Hill Burial Ground (1660)**

⓯ **U.S.S. Constitution ("Old Ironsides")**
Oldest commissioned U.S. warship afloat; also museum

⓰ **Bunker Hill Monument**
Battle on June 17, 1775

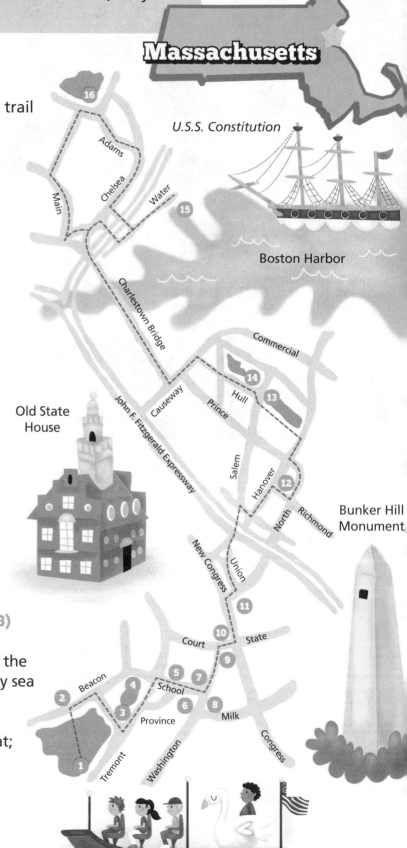

U.S.S. Constitution

Boston Harbor

Old State House

Bunker Hill Monument

Acadia National Park

Acadia National Park, located mostly on an island, is full of the sounds and sights of the sea. Salty waves crash against tumbled, rocky cliffs and boom into Thunder Hole. Whales slide by, and lobster boats haul in the day's catch. Sailboats dart with the wind. Climb 1,530-foot Cadillac Mountain. Take a cold ocean swim.

Maine

Rocky Hideaway!
Find six secret objects along the rugged coast of Maine.

kids' road atlas

Using an Atlas
Pages 4-5
Everglades; Florida; Denver; Colorado;
Newport Beach; California; Tijuana
The adventure begins with a turn of the page!

United States
Page 7
1. AL; 2. AK; 3. AZ; 4. AR; 5. CA; 6. CO; 7. CT; 8. DE;
9. FL; 10. GA; 11. HI; 12. ID; 13. IL; 14. IN; 15. IA;
16. KS; 17. KY; 18. LA; 19. ME; 20. MD; 21. MA;
22. MI; 23. MN; 24. MS; 25. MO; 26. MT; 27. NE;
28. NV; 29. NH; 30. NJ; 31. NM; 32. NY; 33. NC;
34. ND; 35. OH; 36. OK; 37. OR; 38. PA; 39. RI;
40. SC; 41. SD; 42. TN; 43. TX; 44. UT; 45. VT;
46. VA; 47. WA; 48. WV; 49. WI; 50. WY

Alabama
Page 8
Huntsville, Alabama

Alaska
Page 9

Arizona
Page 10
How deep?
40 ÷ 10 = 4 Empire State Buildings (up to 5,500
feet deep)
How long?
191+60-10+17+19=277 miles long (Utah is 270
miles wide)

Arkansas
Page 11 (clockwise from top left)
Fort Smith; Little Rock; Pine Bluff; El Dorado,
Texarkana

California
Page 13
1. Redding; 2. Sequoia; 3. Joshua Tree;
4. Yosemite; 5. Kings Canyon; 6. Death Valley
State motto: "Eureka!"

Colorado
Page 14
B-5 Boulder; A-3 Steamboat Springs;
A-6 Crow River; A-2 Dinosaur National Monument;
B-6 Brush; C-5 Castle Rock

Connecticut
Page 15 (Penguins)

Delaware
Page 16

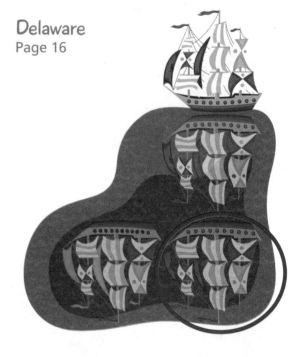

Florida
Page 17
OCEAN and CANOE; PALM and LAMP; PEARS and SPEAR; MELON and LEMON; TEN and NET; SHOE and HOSE; BEARD and BREAD

Georgia
Page 18

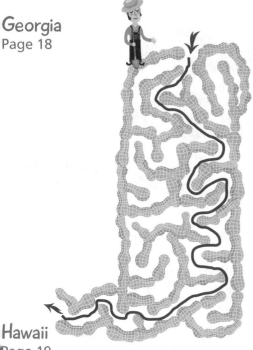

Hawaii
Page 19
Kilauea is an active volcano in Hawaii Volcanoes National Park.

Idaho
Page 20

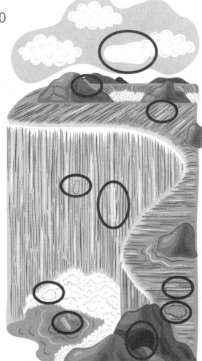

Illinois
Page 21
1. Paris; 2. Beardstown;
3. Sandwich; 4. Rock Falls;
5. Normal; 6. Champaign

Indiana
Page 22
1st – #2 orange; 2nd – #10 red; 3rd – #8 yellow

Iowa
Page 24

1. PIG
2. ROOSTER
3. SHEEP
4. COW
5. GOAT
6. HORSE
7. CHICKEN

More popcorn is produced in Sioux City, Iowa, than in any other place in the world.

Kansas
Page 25

Kentucky
Page 26
(B-4) Louisville; (B-5) Frankfort and Lawrenceburg;
(B-6) Lexington; (C-3) Owensboro; (C-5) Danville;
(C-6) Richmond; (C-8) Pikeville; (D-3) Russellville;
(D-4) Bowling Green; (D-6) London & Williamsburg

Louisiana
Page 27

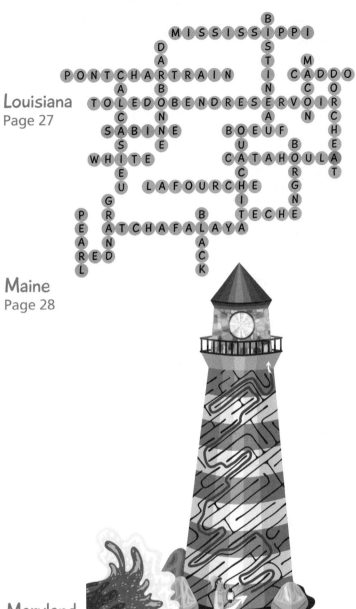

Crossword answers:
MISSISSIPPI
PONTCHARTRAIN CADDO
TOLEDOBENDRESERVOIR
SABINE BOEUF
WHITE CATAHOULA
LAFOURCHE TECHE
PEARL ATCHAFALAYA
GRAND
RED

Maine
Page 28

Maryland
Page 29

He was a prisoner on a British ship.

Massachusetts
Page 31

```
      A D R L P O E
    E X I H O L M E S
  F A N C D E C E R E
  G R R K A H M K R A
  M B A I R E E E W H
  L S L N R E V H A E N
  K E I S K E M N N O L A
  N E O O R L C O T R L L
    N N N B O I R H C Y
      D N C U A N O A
      V K E B D T N I D
      T H O D T R Y E A
    A D A M S Y U
```

Michigan
Page 32

Standard

Minnesota
Page 33

Across: 3. Mille Lacs; 4. Vermilion; 6. Leech
Down: 1. Upper Red; 2. Winnibigoshish;
5. L. Itasca; 6. Lower Red

Mississippi
Page 34

paddlewheel, paddle, pail, palm tree, pants, park, park bench, parking meter, parrot, patch (eye), path, paw, pegleg, pelican, pencil, pepper, periscope, person, picnic, pier, pig, pillow, pineapple, pipe, pirate, plane, plate, pony, poodle, post, puddle

Missouri
Page 35

```
KENTUCKY
      E        A
      N        N
OKLAHOMA  ILLINOIS
      L   O        A
  ARKANSAS  N      S
      H   E  E      A
      O   S  S      S
      M   B         E
      A   R         E
          A
          S
          K
          A
```

Montana
Page 36

New Mexico
Page 41

Nebraska
Page 37

Nevada
Page 38
Las Vegas

New Hampshire
Page 39
ship, ramp, shrimp, man, pines, pear, pie, peas, sheep

New Jersey
Page 40

New York
Page 42-43
mail box, periscope, sailboat on rock, snow boarder, candy cane, chimney on tent, fishing in fire, fire hydrant, dolphin in stream, shoe in tree

North Carolina
Page 44
frog, flashlight, fish, fin (on fish), flamingo, feather, fire or flame, fruit, flower, farmer, fan, flag, flippers, football, fork, foot/feet, face, forehead, fingers, fringe (on towel or blanket), frisbee, four (on flag), fence, funnel, floats, frankfurter

North Dakota
Page 45
1. Bowman; 2. Grand Forks; 3. Valley City; 4. Rugby; 5. Devil's Lake; 6. Carrington

Ohio
Page 47
Findlay, Newark, Ashland, Canton, Whitehall, Springfield, Logan, Athens, Portsmouth, Oxford, Fairborn, Middletown

Oklahoma
Page 48
dine — Enid (B–5); bilead — Idabel (E–8); lowtan — Lawton (E–5); wlassail — Sallisaw (C–8); leekomug — Okmulgee (C–7) ; moungy — Guymon (A–2); usalt — Tulsa (B–7); amimi — Miami (A–8); sheenwa — Shawnee (C–6); talliwerts — Stillwater (B–6)

Oregon
Page 49

Pennsylvania
Page 50

Rhode Island
Page 51
1. red light; 2. redwood; 3. red, white, and blue; 4. see red; 5. Little Red Riding Hood; 6. red carpet; 7. redhead

South Carolina
Page 52

South Dakota
Page 53
The correct order is P, E, O, P, L, E, which spells out PEOPLE

Tennessee
Page 54

Texas
Page 57

Utah
Page 58

```
T G R P P H B L S T I Y B
T L I V E S A R C H E S E
A E B A B R E Z Q R O M A
E N N Q P D I N O S A U R
G C O U L E N N B K I R S
R A O C I F G S G N T A E
O N T A O E X D O Z B D A
G Y F I K G G I L L I B R
G O G B E C W N D A W O S
N N K P N P S H E C V Y N
I S T I R D O U N H R R D
M D A D T E N D S B O C R
A T E J C V P L P A I H A
L X R E O Y T S I M Z S I
F O R S K B R A K N S P V
C A P I T O L R E E F G S
M G I L K B I I J R I A O
A Q R L E B S H O A O N G
O J C R A Y A D C L N W H
C A N Y O N L A N D S P C
T A H H R N I Z L A W M I
R C A L E X S Y T L P I N
S K A E R B R A D E C T C
```

Vermont
Page 59

A = 7; B = 3; C = 1; X = 5
Fact number 5 is false.

Virginia
Page 60

Williamsburg

Washington
Page 62

Father's Day

West Virginia
Page 63

1. Weirton; 2. Ohio; 3. Weston; 4. Potomac;
5. Harpers Ferry; 6. Tug Fork; 7. Kentucky;
8. Charleston
Fact: The New River is America's oldest river.

Wisconsin
Page 64

1. **B**; 2. **A**; 3. **R**; 4. **A**; 5. **B**; 6. **O**; 7. **O**
BARABOO

Wyoming
Page 65

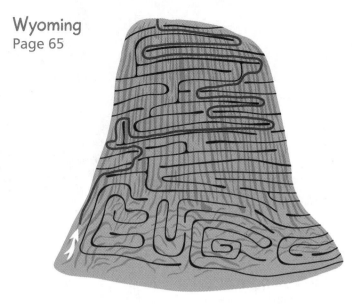

Canada
Page 67

Mexico
Page 68-69

1. Caribbean Sea; 2. Tijuana; 3. Tabasco;
4. Tortilla; 5. Rio Grande; 6. Acapulco; 7. Mexicali;
8. Chihuahua; 9. Pacific Ocean; 10. Guatemala;
11. Ciudad Juárez; 12. El Paso; 13. Belize;
14. Hermosillo
"Mexicans were once known as the men of corn."

are we there yet?

Page 73

Page 74
1. C; 2. A; 3. H; 4. F; 5. B;
6. D; 7. E; 8. G; 9. I

Page 75

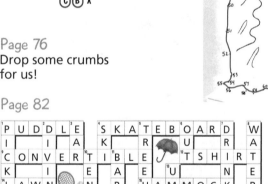

Page 77

Page 76
Drop some crumbs
for us!

Page 82

Page 83
table, tablecloth, tackle box, tag, tape, taxi, teapot,
teddy bear, teeth, telephone, ten (on a price tag),
tennis racket, tent, thermometer, thermos, thumb,
ticket, tie, tools, toothbrush, towel, toys, trees, tricycle,
trunk, T-shirt, Tuesday (on calendar), turtleneck,
tuxedo, and typewriter

Page 84
1. B; 2. J; 3. D; 4. K; 5. M; 6. F; 7. G; 8. O; 9. C; 10. A;
11. H; 12. E; 13. I; 14. L; 15. N

Page 85
1. steering wheel; 2. hood; 3. accelerator; 4. trunk;
5. windshield; 6. brake; 7. dashboard; 8. wheel;
9. gearshift; 10. engine; 11. headlight; 12. bumper;
13. muffler; 14. battery

Page 86

Page 87
1. beach umbrella is inside out; 2. lifeguard is facing the
wrong way; 3. man in water is dressed in evening wear;
4. fisherman is fishing with a rake; 5. skiier is skiing
without a boat; 6. people warming up at a campfire;
7. golfer on the beach; 8. people playing volleyball
with a football; 9. sailboat has an upside-down sail;
10. in-line skater on the sand

Page 89
1. park hours on sign are only at night; 2. missing
rungs on slide ladder; 3. alligator in the fountain;
4. pterodactyl in the sky; 5. inner tube slide spills out
onto a golf tee; 6. big pair of glasses on the inner tube
slide ramp; 7. queen in the lifeguard chair; 8. ice skater
skating on the pool; 9. bed in the pool; 10. playing card
lying on the deck; 11. herd of sheep in the picnic area.

Page 90

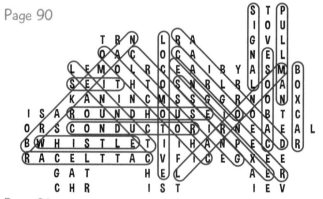

Page 91
1. buttercup; 2. pansy; 3. snapdragon; 4. carnation;
5. foxglove; 6. daisy; 7. cowslip; 8. goldenrod

Page 92
Michelle trail 1, Juan trail 2, and Keisha trail 3.

Page 93

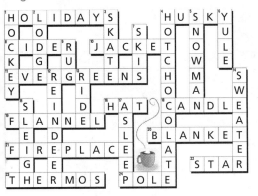

Crossword solution:
HOLIDAYS / HUSKY
COOK / SKIS / OTC / NULE
CIDER / JACKET / TCHI / U
KEG / U / TI / HOM / LE
EVERGREENS / HMA / S
Y / EI / OA / W
SID / HAT / CANDLE
FLANNEL / ISL / OO / EA
ED / L / OT / NE
FIREPLACE / EE / BLANKET
GE / E / AT / E
THERMOS / POLE / STAR

Page 94

The man in the convertible wasn't telling the truth because he couldn't have driven from Salt Lake City in Utah to Chattanooga in Tennessee in 12 hours.

Page 95

Page 97

Say this three times fast: She sells seashells by the seashore.

Page 98

1. dog; 2. cat; 3. cow; 4. toad; 5. duck; 6. goat; 7. crow; 8. goose; 9. mouse; 10. horse; 11. robin; 12. rabbit; 13. raccoon; 14. squirrel

Page 100

Page 103

1. F; 2. G; 3. E; 4. D; 5. H; 6. A; 7. I; 8. C; 9. B; 10. J

Page 104-105

Page 106

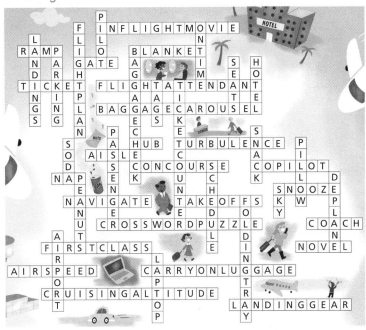

Page 107

1. large bike's seat is backwards; 2. yield sign is upside-down; 3. spokes missing on small bike; 4. center line on road is weaving; 5. tree growing in middle of road; 6. zebra; 7. airplane flying upside-down; 8. sun in front of cloud; 9. cow in distance is as big as the house; 10. no straps on backpack

Page 108

1. You can buy a necklace, polished rock, postcard, wind-up toy, and candy for exactly 205 tickets.
2. Or, you can buy a key ring, candy, giant pencil, and postcard for exactly 205 tickets.

Page 109

The Sleep Inn is the correct hotel.

Page 110

Page 115

1. peanut butter and jelly; 2. taco; 3. macaroni and cheese; 4. spaghetti; 5. hamburger

Page 116

1. ark; 2. ship; 3. raft; 4. canoe; 5. yacht; 6. kayak;
7. barge 8. tugboat; 9. gondola; 10. sailboat;
11. submarine; 12. windsurfer; 13. aircraft carrier

Page 117

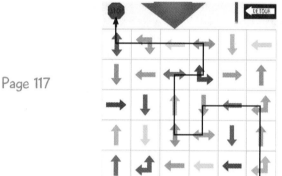

Page 118

Page 119

The lady couldn't have a son. She explained that she only had a sister. That sister's father (her father) had a wife (her mother) whose mother (her grandmother) had a great granddaughter (her daughter, since her sister has no children) who has a twin sister (also her daughter) who has no brother. If her daughters have no brother, she couldn't have a son. Also, North Carolina isn't the Peach State, Georgia is.

Page 121

Skiers B and H are exactly alike.

Page 122

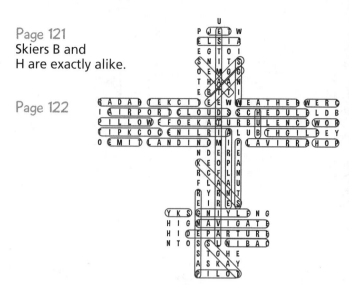

Page 123

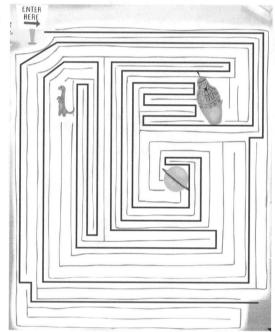

Page 124

Page 125

How does a country vote for a new symbol? They have a flag poll.

Page 132

1. Picture Park 2. Travel Time; 3. Wacky water park;
4. You're bugging ME!; 5. On the Right Track;
6. Bloomers; 7. Happy Camper?; 8. Barnyard SCRAMBLE;
9. Travel Journal

Are you there yet?

coast-to-coast games

Page 138

Cinder cone	5	Lava	3
Crater	1	Magma	2
Eruption	6	Vent	8
Gas and ash	7	Volcanic bombs	4

Page 139

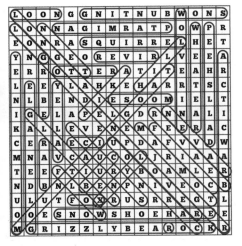

Page 142

Black bear	Antelope
Geysers	Bighorn sheep
Bison	Yellowstone Falls
Mammoth Hot Springs	Bald Eagle
Grizzly bear	Old Faithful
Moose	Paint Pots
Elk (Wapiti)	Beaver

Page 143

River
Table
Potato
Garden
Chair
Clock
Wristwatch
River
Bread
Bed
Violin, guitar
Macaroni
Corn
Gloves

Page 144

Gum wrapper	1 month
Orange peel	3 months
Pop can	200-500 years
Styrofoam cup	Over 500 years
Rubber tire	Over 500 years
Plastic pop rings	Over 500 years
Glass bottle	1,000,000 years

Page 145

```
            G O L F
  I C E S K A T E
          S K I
      R I D E
          T E N N I S
        S A I L
        H I K E
      B O A T
  W A T E R S K I
```

Page 146

12 states

New York	Indiana	Wyoming
New Jersey	Illinois	Utah
Pennsylvania	Iowa	Nevada
Ohio	Nebraska	California

Page 147

```
              C     A H W A H N E E
    M E A D O W           A
    E       N       S     L       E
    R   Y O S E M I T E F A L L S
    C   O     E       E   D     C
  F E R N     Q       R   O   P A S S
    D         U       R O A M     P
              C       O     E   H I K E
    M A R I P O S A         T     D
          M   A         L   A     Y
          P   M O U N T A I N     T   H
  T R A I L   N         K     N   T   A
    O     N   T U O L U M N E   V A L E
    C     G   R             U     I   A
    K         E A G L E     T   P E A K
              E                     W
```

Page 148

CARAMEL	CAROUSEL
CARAWAY	CARPENTER
CARBURETOR	CARPET
CARDS	CARRIAGE
CARDINAL	CARROT
CAREFUL	CARTON
CARNIVAL	

Page 149

Disneyland
Knott's Berry Farm
Hollywood
Farmer's Market
Sea World
Rancho La Brea Tar Pits
Hollywood Bowl
Six Flags Magic Mountain
Universal Studios Hollywood
Queen Mary
Beverly Hills
Rose Bowl
Autry Museum of the American West
NBC Studios
Griffith Park Observatory
The Coliseum

Page 150

The middle section in the left column matches the bottom section in the right column.

Ages of trees:	8	10
	11	6
	7	11

Page 151

Giraffe	Lion	Kangaroo
Elephant	Zebra	Hippopotamus
Cheetah	Monkey	

Page 152

1. Indianapolis, Oklahoma City
2. Annapolis, Maryland
3. Baton Rouge, Louisiana
4. Lincoln, Nebraska
5. Nashville, Tennessee

(continued on page 218)

Page 152 (continued from page 217)

6. Dover, Delaware; Honolulu, Hawaii; Indianapolis, Indiana; Oklahoma City, Oklahoma

7. Juneau, Alaska (Honolulu, Hawaii can be reached by car from other parts of Oahu Island)

8. Sacramento, California; Saint Paul, Minnesota; Salem, Oregon; Salt Lake City, Utah; Santa Fe, New Mexico; Springfield, Illinois

9. Santa Fe, New Mexico; established in 1610

10. Pierre (South Dakota)

Page 153

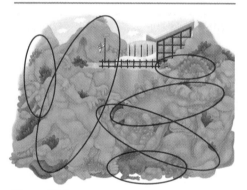

Page 154

<table>
<tr><td>E</td><td>K</td><td>C</td><td>L</td><td>I</td><td>F</td><td>F</td></tr>
<tr><td>K</td><td>C</td><td>A</td><td>M</td><td>P</td><td>O</td><td>T</td></tr>
<tr><td>I</td><td>O</td><td>N</td><td>W</td><td>A</td><td>L</td><td>L</td></tr>
<tr><td>B</td><td>R</td><td>Y</td><td>C</td><td>E</td><td>D</td><td>O</td></tr>
<tr><td>Z</td><td>I</td><td>O</td><td>N</td><td>D</td><td>E</td><td>R</td></tr>
<tr><td>S</td><td>U</td><td>N</td><td>H</td><td>I</td><td>K</td><td>E</td></tr>
<tr><td>T</td><td>O</td><td>W</td><td>E</td><td>R</td><td>I</td><td>M</td></tr>
</table>

Page 155

Dam	Ring
Lamb	Sing or Swing
Feet	Mouth
Beet	South
Ball	Book
Mall	Cook
Clocks	Bike
Blocks	Hike
Light	Jump
Fight	Pump

Page 156

Page 157

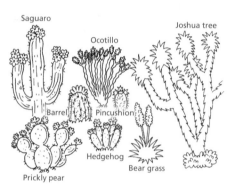

Saguaro · Ocotillo · Joshua tree · Barrel · Pincushion · Hedgehog · Bear grass · Prickly pear

Page 158

Arizona-Sonora Desert Museum	5
Barrio Historico	7
Fort Huachuca	4
Kitt Peak Observatory	1
O.K. Corral	3
Old Tucson	6
Pima Air & Space Museum	2
Tombstone	8

Page 160

Page 162

Cowboy

Oil Well

Capitol Building

Ranches

Old West

Gilcrease Museum

Horses

Echo

Page 164

arbol	10	tree
burro	6	donkey
casa	1	house
gato	5	cat
iglesia	3	church, mission
mano	13	hand
niña	12	girl
niño	15	boy
pelo	11	hair
pelota	14	ball
perro	4	dog
piñata	9	candy-filled toy
serape	8	shawl
sol	2	sun
sombrero	7	hat
zapatos	16	shoes

Page 165

Minnesota	Wisconsin
Iowa	Illinois
Missouri	Kentucky
Arkansas	Tennessee
Louisiana	Mississippi

Page 166

Pan	Pickaxe	Shovel
Burro	Miner	Bag of gold

Page 168

Tube 2

Page 169

Bird	Worm
Dog	Bone
Rabbit	Carrot
Bear	Fish
Otter	Shellfish
Giraffe	Leaves
Ape	Banana
Elephant	Peanuts

Page 170

Man with a pack	Lake Huron
Cucumber	Lake Michigan
Wolf head	Lake Superior

Page 171

A	Apple	N	Necklace
B	Ball	O	Orange
C	Candy (sucker)	P	Pail (and shovel)
D	Doll	Q	Quoits
E	Elephant	R	Race car
F	Flashlight	S	Sled
G	Goldfish	T	Tom-tom
H	Hobbyhorse	U	Unicycle
I	Ice cream	V	Valentine
J	Jet (airplane)	W	Wristwatch
K	Keys	X	Xylophone
L	Locomotive	Y	Yo-yo
M	Mitt	Z	Zebra

Page 173

Parts of a horse:

Barrel	7
Chest	10
Fetlock	8
Forelock	12
Haunch	3
Hock	5
Hoof	9
Mane	1
Nostrils	11
Tail	4
Thigh	6
Withers	2

True or false:

T   F   T   F   T   T   F

Page 175

STATE
1. California
2. Missouri
3. New York
4. Colorado
5. Illinois
6. New Mexico
7. Pennsylvania
8. Tennessee
9. Virginia
10. Washington D.C.

LANDMARK
Pueblos (6)
Statue of Liberty (3)
Grand Ole Opry (8)
Lincoln Memorial (10)
Hollywood (1)
Colonial Williamsburg (9)
Field Museum (5)
Gateway Arch (2)
Liberty Bell (7)
Pikes Peak (4)

Page 176

Message: Have a good time

Page 177

Left to right:
Top row — Idaho, Nebraska, Illinois, West Virginia, New Hampshire
Row 2 — California, Texas, Mississippi, Florida

Page 178

Paddlewheel
Flag on prow
Smokestack
Flag on pilot house
First deck 3rd window from right
Second deck near window
Second deck railing
Windows on pilot house
Color of flag on stern

Page 181

These are two possible answers:

RAN	RAN
RAIN	RANG
TRAIN	GRANT
STRAIN	GRANTS
STARING	RATINGS
STARTING	STARTING

Page 182

CNN
OMNI
MARTA
BRAVES
CAPITOL
SIX FLAGS
CYCLORAMA
M.L. KING SITE

Page 184

THRILLS

Page 185

Shark
Roller Coaster
Airboat
Waterski
Dolphins
Movie Stunt
Balloon
Alligator
Castle
Beaches

Page 186

Alligators
Spoonbill
Airboat
Sawgrass
Crane
Turtle
Snake

Page 187

Upside down:
Pelican
Rocket
Space Shuttle
Turtle
Swimming duck

Astronaut on outside of rocket
Heron sitting on rocket
Fish swimming on land
Cattails growing on bottom of stems

Page 188

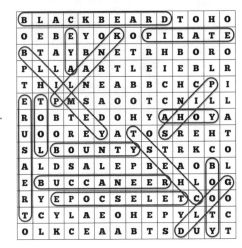

Page 190

Alexander Graham Bell	5
Telephone	
George Washington Carver	2
Peanut products	
Pierre and Marie Curie	8
Radium	
George Eastman	10
Roll film for cameras	
Thomas Alva Edison	1
Electric lights	

(continued on page 220)

Page 190 (continued from page 219)

Benjamin Franklin	4
Electricity	
Guglielmo Marconi	9
Radio	
Samuel F.B. Morse	6
Telegraph, Morse Code	
Eli Whitney	7
Cotton gin	
Orville and Wilbur Wright	3
Airplane (sustained flight)	

Page 191

Apothecary	7	Medicine
Baker	4	Pie
Blacksmith	2	Horseshoe
Cabinetmaker	9	Chair
Cooper	3	Barrel
Milliner	6	Hat, bonnet
Peruke maker	5	Wig
Silversmith	8	Candlestick
Wheelwright	1	Wheel

Page 193

Page 194

Page 195

Washington Monument
Bureau of Engraving and Printing
Vietnam Veterans' Memorial
National Air & Space Museum
The White House
Arlington National Cemetery
Smithsonian Institution (main building)
National Zoological Park

Page 196

40 triangles

Page 197

Would use:
  candle
  plain coat and hat
  mule and plow
  buggy
  button
  plain dress
Would not use:
  Automobile
  Zipper
  Electricity
  Electric lamp
  Telephone
  Camera

Page 199

3	bears
7	oceans
10	fingers
9	planets
5	quintet
50	U.S. states
12	dozen
13	flag stripes
7	continents
4	lucky clover leaves
6	half dozen
2	pair
13	baker's dozen
13	original colonies
18	age to vote
4	corners in a square

Page 200

The second and fourth cannons from the left match

Page 201

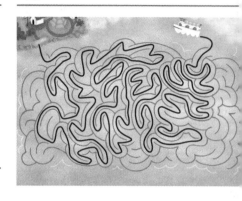

Page 202

27 blocks

Page 204

Bay	11
Canal	10
Cape	13
Channel	2
Dam	4
Delta	7
Inlet	9
Island	15
Lake	8
Ocean	12
Peninsula	3
Reservoir	1
River	5
Sound	14
Tributary	6

Page 205

Plimoth Plantation
Mayflower
Plymouth Rock
Pilgrim Village
Forefathers' Monument
Myles Standish Monument
Pilgrim Hall Museum
Old Fort House

Page 207

Canoe on the shore
Sailboat in the clouds
Moose head in the water
Lobster, fish, and clam in the rocks

Populations are from the 2010 U.S. Census or other national censuses.